CW01187124

BACOPA

Literary Review 2021

Writers Alliance of Gainesville

Writers Alliance

ISBN: 9798465324267

Printed in the United States of America

Cover Art: Grayson May, https://graysonmay.com
Cover/Text/Layout Design: Richard G. Skinner

Fonts:

Calisto MT

An old-style serif typeface designed for the Monotype Corporation foundry in 1986 by Ron Carpenter, a British typographer, Calisto MT is intended to function as a typeface for both body text and display text.

Adobe Jensen Pro

An old-style serif typeface drawn for Adobe Systems by its chief type designer Robert Slimbach, Adobe Jensen Pro's Roman styles are based on a text face cut by Nicolas Jenson in Venice around 1470; its italics are based on those created by Ludovico Vicentino degli Arrighi fifty years later.

From the Editors

I love the stars because they flicker. I love the stars because they recede.
I love the stars because they trace perfect circles if you plant yourself
on a hill and let the aperture stay open all night, exposed.
—Shana Ross, "If Betelgeuse Explodes, I Will Be Sad"

As we assemble each edition of *Bacopa Literary Review*, we look for themes. One over-arching focus in both 2020 and 2021 is grief. This theme, pervasive in every aspect of our lives for the last year and a half as we all endure the COVID-19 pandemic, is clearly present in this year's journal. But some of the other themes this year have surprised us, a fascinating and uplifting set of motifs employed in ways as simultaneously jarring and consoling as the image of the little bird in Emily Dickinson's famous poem "'Hope' is the thing with feathers," who *sings the tune without the words—/ And never stops—at all— / / And sweetest—in the Gale—is heard.*

It would be easy to let grief overwhelm us, in times like these, and some of our selections reflect on that ease. There is the dark, all-encompassing existential agony over a family tragedy expressed in Alec Kissoondyal's "Smudge." Its complement, the long slog through the initial stages of grief and into something approximating the rest of life for those left behind, is portrayed in Shuly Cawood's "Not Naming It." There is also the gentle, even humorous sense of resignation and peace-making with grief expressed in both Janet Marugg's fictional vignette "Lila's Last Day" and Lora Straub's nonfiction essay "A Fragile Inheritance."

In part as acknowledgement of the need to face and work through the individual and collective sorrows COVID-19 has wrought, we open this year's collection with Megan Wildhood's probing, elegiac "Oh. There is No Going Back." Wildhood's poem takes up grief and turns it around like a many-faceted gem, examining its dark surfaces and acknowledging the ways it impacts even our memory and understanding of life before the grieving time: *the first time I remembered the Before world and it was full / of holes.*

But we've noticed plenty of other shared themes in this year's *Bacopa*. Most are riffs on the great concerns of human existence, and thereby of most literature—love, joy, struggle, pain, pride, humility, endurance. One motif across genres surprised us, though. Birds—those "things with feathers" and wings.

We invite you to keep an eye out for them as you read your way through this year's offerings. Some, such as the baby birds in Kissoondyal's "Smudge," Adam Knight's "Little Bird," and the small bird that crashes into a window at the opening of Elizabeth Christopher's "Dream Catcher," show up as emblems of fragility, loss, and, yes, grief. Timi Sanni's pained, prayerful poem "Orison" even presents us with the antithesis to Dickinson's eternal, undaunted feathered singer: *the bird/ of hope folding its wings, its hollow bones// crushing as they welcome the uncanny force/ of darkness.* These birds, and some of the others that flit through the pages that follow, are creatures of night, of darkness or at least a liminal space—the edge of shadow where darkness meets, commingles with light. They remind us that time flows unceasing and life proceeds in all its shades—from drudgery and weariness, pain and fear, through excitement, exultation, and joy—and all those shades are certainly represented in a myriad of tints and tones.

Artists are grappling with the reality that humanity as a whole, the world over, is undergoing a tremendous cataclysm of collective loss and mourning, at this moment of history. People are mourning lost friends and loved ones, lost jobs and businesses, lost opportunities and experiences—from students missing out on graduations and other rites of passage, to families delaying having children, partners delaying marriage, and so much more. For many of us, the pandemic delayed our ability to be physically present with each other, to collectively express and process these many and varied sorrows. For too many of us, a long-delayed process of grieving has only recently begun in earnest.

Our shadow birds remind us, as Shana Ross's First Prize poem quoted in the epigraph above so presciently puts it, *When you live in too much light you cannot see the stars/yet they exist.*

But most of *Bacopa 2021*'s birds fly in the other direction, and beautifully so, as exemplified by the powerful mythical bird that lends its name to Sergio Ortiz's fierce "Yo soy el Fénix." Birds—strong, fierce and joyful—are central characters in both William Nuessle's "Hero's Eyes" and this year's Fiction First Prize winner, Tomas Baiza's "Huitzilin." Flight, uplift, release—these themes are woven through every category of writing. Though too many of us are still inside the edge of the shadow, many here at home and around the world are beginning to see the gilded limning of the other side.

We hope you will find yourself lifted, energized, and inspired as we were by the tremendous outpouring of talent and creativity we received for our 2021 journal. May we move onward and upward together, like the tiny winged warriors of "Huitzilin," out of the global shroud of this pandemic and into the blaze of a new day dawning. May we be so blessed as to know the joy and triumph that surges through the closing line of Baiza's magical tale: *And so, I become light.*

—J.N. Fishhawk & Mary Bast

Bacopa Literary Review 2021 Prizes

FICTION

First Prize

Huitzilin / page 156 / Tomas Baiza

Second Prize

The Vanishing Heart / page 3 / Fern F. Musselwhite

CREATIVE NONFICTION

First Prize

And The Road Goes On Forever / page 140 / Gerald O. Ryan

Second Prize

A Fragile Inheritance / page 59 / Lora Straub

POETRY

First Prize

If Betelgeuse Explodes, I Will Be Sad / page 28 / Shana Ross

Second Prize

Key Lime Pie / page 164 / Shoshauna Shy

PROSE POETRY

First Prize

car wash orgasmic whirl / page 143 / Nicole Farmer

Second Prize

Grenadine / page 10 / Les Epstein

Contents

FICTION

CREATIVE NONFICTION

PROSE POETRY

POETRY

Oh. There is No Going Back.

Megan Wildhood

the last time I walked barefaced into a building
the last time I rollicked in a crowd
the last time I smiled at a stranger and the stranger knew it
life is so terrible
the first time I smiled at a stranger whether the stranger knew it or not
the first time I crossed the street when a person, stranger or not,
was approaching
the first time I washed my hands for the length of the happy birthday song
life is so holy
the last time I blew out birthday candles on a cake surrounded by friends
the first time I had to calculate my own age
the last time I felt my own age
is life so terrible?
the first time I felt age
the last time I thought aging was guaranteed
the first time I remembered the Before world and it was full
of holes
is life not holy?
life is so holy, too holy, and so terrible,
too terrible to be just
an afterimage

Muddle

E.D. Lloyd-Kimbrel

June the twenty-ninth is International Mud Day. I do not know who decides these things.

A great advocate of mud, I was adept as a child at making mud pies. All about process, not consumption. I did not just pack mud into a pie plate. Oh no. I with high intent cross-hatched wild onion stems atop and crimped the inner edge with my thumb. Eventually even that was insufficient because even an exquisite mud pie is still not fully and truly a pie. For a pie to be a pie it must be baked.

And so, one still and quiet summer afternoon not too heavy with heat when I was at the age of four years or so, after I had watered with my dearly dented tin watering can the good dirt spot under the shade of the little laurel grove in the backyard and stick-stirred it into mud of an admirable consistency, I hand-scooped and firmly patted the dark dough into the metal pan, thumb-printed the circumference, crisscrossed the onion stems on top with some sour-grass leaves in the center as special decoration, traversed the yard, marched up the back porch steps into the empty kitchen (taking care not to let the screen door slam), opened the oven door, placed the pan on the rack, closed the oven door, and turned the oven dial the way I had seen my mother do. A gas oven. With automatic pilot. (Did I mention I was four years old or so?)

Imagine the smell of burnt dirt.

With just the merest whiff of fried *allium canadense*.

Such scents, like as flowers for bees, attracted my mother.

Like Queen Victoria, she was not amused.

Fiction Second Prize

The Vanishing Heart

Fern F. Musselwhite

The crisp white lab coats surround her with their earnestness, a thin veil for greedy curiosity.

Sophie surveys the conference table and tries to recall the last question from the tall man with the thinning gray hair sitting across from her. What does she remember from that day, that night? From the week before, the months before? What changed?

Nothing she'd noticed. Jake had been sick with the latest variant, but so had millions. Fifteen years had passed since the last coronavirus scorched the planet. This time, when the human wildfire spread, the doctors were ready. People went to work, flew around the world. Lived. Physicians like these around the table fought the new enemy with better weaponry. In weeks they had treatments. In months a vaccine.

Jake had been in New York covering a story. They thought he'd contracted the virus traveling home. He'd tested positive, stayed in bed a few days with a cough and slight fever. Fluids, rest, Tylenol. He'd bounced back in a week with no obvious residual effects. Sophie had avoided infection.

One morning she woke before the alarm. In the sleepy blue gray dawn, she rested a hand on Jake's arm and watched him breathe. The dark folds of the sheet rising and falling with the quiet cadence of slumber.

Light streams in the third-floor windows of the conference room. Sophie hears a garbage truck lifting a dumpster into the air. The squeak of brakes, the squeal of hydraulics, the crash of waste into the back of the truck. The slam of the lid as the truck releases the dumpster. She pictures the entire process, yet she jumps at the bang of metal against metal. The end of the ordeal.

"Effortless," she says.

They squint, furrow, the lab coats. "Come again?" one says.

"Effortless. His breathing that morning. It was effortless. Normal. Then it just stopped." She looks around the table, as if asking the physicians for an explanation.

She'd been lying on her side, thinking about the quarterly financial report due for her 10:30 meeting, watching the dust dance in the air. After a moment

—was it a minute, maybe five?—she heard the silence. The absence of breathing. A chill brushed her skin.

"Jake?" she whispered as she rubbed his arm. "Jake?" again, but with force. Finally, "Jake!"

She threw off the covers, lunged for her phone. Ran to unlock the front door while pleading with the dispatcher to hurry please God hurry. Chest compressions. Jake, stay with me. Jake.

The lab coats exchange glances, peer at their notes. One musters, "And before?" Sophie looks past him at the carafe of coffee on the credenza, the steam curling out of the black plastic lid. The vapor fades, disappears against the gray wall. "Nothing out of the ordinary. Like I told the doctors before the autopsy. He was fine. And no family history."

They nod. Not that there would be a history of this.

After the service and the departures of friends and family, the questions began. The autopsy showed not that the heart had stopped. It showed no heart at all.

"So he was feeling fine when he went to bed. Talked to you. And then in the morning he stops breathing and can't be resuscitated. Correct?"

"Yes."

They type and scribble. More squinting and furrowing. The rest wait for the tall man to dismiss this woman. To acknowledge she has nothing to give.

At the hospital they'd cracked open Jake's chest. As they continued to shock and compress, to strain and rotate hands, they noticed Jake's heart was shrinking. Dwindling before their eyes until nothing remained. Nothing to shock or compress. Gone.

The lab coats return to the autopsy report summary before them: Forty-two-year-old white male with no history of heart disease. How could they explain a vanishing heart? What makes a heart disappear, leaving everything else behind?

"Thank you for coming in, Ms. Grant." The tall man rises, reaches across the table. Sophie takes his hand, warm and dry. She wonders how he can be so calm. How anyone can.

The lab coats meet with other lab coats. They study Jake's body, his medical records. They assemble at conferences in hotel ballrooms, eat buttery croissants, watch presentations. They break into small groups in the afternoon, share whiskeys in the bar in the evening, trade theories. But no one from New York to Los Angeles, from London to Tel Aviv, from Sydney to Tokyo to Beijing, no one can explain how Jake Grant's heart vanished.

Six months later another heart disappears. A 68-year-old woman dies in a small village in France. She has no connection to Jake Grant. Three weeks later a teenager in Idaho. A week after that, deaths in Barcelona, Johannesburg. The windswept, rocky coast of Cape Breton Island. Soon thousands of hearts will vanish. Sleeping, running, buying groceries. The lab coats find no obvious trigger, no pattern. No way to predict who will be next. The counted become countless. The squinting and furrowing stop. The eyes are wide open.

Two years after Jake's death a discovery in Stockholm. An enzyme shared by all humans mutates with the virus. It is this mutation, the lab coats believe, that causes heart tissue alone to shrink and disappear. They've seen no other ill effects of the mutated enzyme, but they begin testing. Everyone who had the virus, babies born to infected parents.

Around the world protocol dictates that every child born is tested for the mutated enzyme. The lab coats confirm the mutation is spreading. In less than a generation, every infant tests positive. The clock ticks. The lab coats wrinkle.

Wind whips across the desert and rattles the thin walls of the small clinic. The doctor, a petite woman with brown eyes and the sinew of a lioness, looks out the window as tumbleweeds roll by. She never thought they were real, these brown balls of dried thistle, these fuzzy characters from childhood cartoons. But this is not the Bronx, and last night's windstorm piled them behind her Corolla, making her late this morning.

"Run it again," she tells the nurse. Of course it will come back positive. They probably didn't get enough saliva the first time. The doctor looks around the cramped room at the stained floor and chipped cabinets. The government surplus examination table and chair. She knows they're lucky to have tests at all.

"Same, negative." The nurse hands her the test paper. Bad batch? "No," says the nurse. "We've used this batch all week."

"Open a new box."

Third test, then calls to the hospital 70 miles away. The child is a bright-eyed, healthy girl. They receive a new box the next day. The baby tests negative.

The first lab coat arrives from New York the following Monday. Two more from San Francisco on Tuesday. Each begins cautiously with the child, but beneath the placid face of science each wrestles to temper the fury raging in the mind. The urgency of discovery, cure. Salvation in its basest form. The light of creation arising from a petri dish.

Within a week the medical community around the world buzzes. The baby's mother understands the significance, but the lab coats can't convince her to submit her child to their entreaties. Please, they beg her. For humanity.

But the testing, what you will do to her. Blood samples, bright lights. A procession of masked strangers passing her along in wonder. Marveling at the tiny *objet d'art*; forgetting she has a name and a soul. And the media encamped outside our door. She shakes her head. Not my baby. Leave us be.

Her doctor mediates the conversation. She knows the good that could come, but her loyalty is to her patient. She knows what they will do to the child. Nothing dangerous, but too much. She stares out the window as the lab coats show their colorful slides to the mother. Bar graphs of royal blue and emerald green and the burning orange of sunset. Outside the desert is beige and the sky a hazy white. This mother lives in the soft colors of the blowing sand. She will not give her baby to the blinding hues of the city.

With time she relents. She thinks of her mother, gone. Not from the vanishing heart but breast cancer. Still, she sees her daughter's future and fears her own absence. Perhaps a few tests. A few visits to the city.

The media learn of little Rose and stories ensue. Miracle baby. Could this be the answer? Will she save us?

She does. The lab coats use Rose's Enzyme, as it's named, to create a new vaccine to prevent the vanishing heart. Deaths stop. Fear subsides. The lab coats unfurrow. They pause their squinting.

On her 22nd birthday, diploma in hand, Rose packs her car, kisses her mother's cheek. She heads east to a university town green with maple trees and the shimmering streets of August heat. A month later she spends a Saturday morning driving north to pay a visit to a woman still haunted by the vanishing. Still longing for the return of that beating heart.

"So nice to meet you finally," Sophie says as she welcomes Rose. She brushes a lock of gray hair from her face as she closes the door. The emails, the photos, the calls, none prepared her for the emotions. The momentary flush of hope, warming the skin until the chill of memory, of reality, extinguishes the glow. For all this child brought, Jake remains beyond Sophie's reach.

Sophie serves lemonade and brownies. A mix, but rich dark chocolate. They sit on the patio at a small table Sophie bought years ago. Two chairs, one filled on a rare afternoon by a friend. More often a chair sits empty as Sophie watches the sun set over the neighbor's fence.

They speak of graduation, retirement, the desert and the East. Of the vanishing heart.

“You saved the world you know,” Sophie says. “You prevented pain, sorrow. It’s quite a thing you did.”

Rose blushes, shakes her head. “It wasn’t me. My mom made it happen.”

“She allowed it to happen. But it was you.”

Shadows lengthen across the grass. Ice melts and lemonade pales as light streams through the glass. Sophie watches a fiery red maple leaf tumble across the yard. A life succumbed, so radiant in death.

“But I couldn’t save Jake,” Rose says. “There are so many people I couldn’t help.” She twists a napkin in her hands. If only if only if only. In the years to come the words will consume her, propel her. Haunt her.

“Is that why you found me? Why you’re here?”

Rose squirms in her chair. “Maybe. Yes.”

Sophie remembers the last morning with Jake. The sound of his breathing. The familiar cowlick jutting across his left ear. The terror that filled her heart as his disappeared. The lab coats. The years of research. And finally this young woman. She takes Rose’s hand and grips the warmth of young life, of goodness, vigor. In the long shade of a dwindling day, Sophie feels the hope to be born in the dawns to follow.

“I lost Jake when his heart vanished. But my heart is here. Safe. You gave me that. It is enough.”

Rose nods. She is relieved, surefooted in her path, heady with confidence.

They embrace at the door and promise to visit again. Rose unlocks her car, slides behind the wheel, places her bag on the passenger’s seat. The crisp white lab coat hangs in its plastic in the back.

She squints, furrows her brow.

Pear Blossom

Mendocino, California

Frederick Livingston

this tree could be dead
or dreaming

dark gnarled bark
ringed in rows
of holes where
long-flown birds
searched for worms
in depths of winter . . .

until sudden flush
of blooms consume
lichen-crusted branches
with white five-petal
promises of summer
swollen eat-me sweets

well before
glee-green leaves
greet sun
spun into sugar
proving dreams
precede the means

where is fear
of late-season frost
shattering this frail unfurling?
where are the rations
siloed inside against
lingering winter?

here instead is
chirping of birds returning
daffodils erupting
at the tree's feet
and a question
whispered sweet on cold breeze:

what would the Earth look like
if all of us had such courage
to offer our most tender selves
not only when spring is certain
but when we can no longer bear
our hunger for a more fruitful world?

Prose Poetry Second Prize

Grenadine

Les Epstein

My glasses steam half-fogged as another Sunday arrives with a howl. It's a howl and a rattle and a pound on our panes, right where the cats sit watching spits of ice—a curb to any chance of getting off this mountain.

I've to scurry up to our Salem. (One with its own infamous trials.) It's time to offer my arm for its first blast of a frosty liquid, which television seers say should hold off the spiked menace now chewing its way through venues like Toledo, Memphis, and Omaha.

What a damned chewing show.

Lungs snarled, town after town infected, numbers rising, Italy crushed, old people stolen away to somewhere. One bit of flying snot in Salem could cause my demise.

I have dealt with dangers before. I was told never to use the Penn Station john. Danger lurks within those stalls. But I shattered the rule in '86 after busing in on the Adirondack Trails. Some things just cannot be helped. We were all safe, those of us who streamed into urinals. Outside, a man at the subway entrance shouted at me. "Jews," he said as I walked past. "I hate Jews," he screamed in my ear and showed me his knife, his spit splattering my glasses in tommy-gun fury.

We line up on the floor where Alice Cooper once played his hopping horror show, his savage vaudeville my father once said I should fear. But it came complete with snakes and guillotines and grand top hats. What's to fear? Men in top hats, of course.

There is a folding chair for rest and recuperation after the jab. It's a metal one certain to provide comfort and support for your stunned body. "What could be bad about him?" I hear one man say to a phone. "He says he likes beer." My arm throbs; I plan a search for a green taper.

More ice falls that night. So I huddle up with an ancient tabby, stripped of his spring by arthritis and fading kidneys. Together we'll knock fears adrift all the while peeking out a widening crag in our unraveling afghan cave.

I'd like to welcome all for a few drinks, perhaps tonic or swinging "dirty Shirley." I never keep beer. Only shadows may enter the house. So I'll quiver from a swift and icy Shirley Temple, relish a liquid blessed with explosive little pops; I shall be armed with grenadine.

Lila's Last Day

Janet Marugg

Lila is long past the age of cures, long into being sick with poisonous secrets. She had wanted her mind to deteriorate at the same rate as her body, spare her too much time to remember, reflect and regret. Memories tax her body more than arthritic joints and aged muscles.

She spreads Arnie's ashes under the wisteria and sits on the bench under the drapes of lavender blossoms. The bench is rusting wrought iron. Maintenance of inanimate objects is never a priority. That much she had shared with Arnie when he was alive, caring for living things in the garden.

When she leaves, Lila will miss the garden most. It is a sanctuary that she helped build with Arnie. "With our bodies, for our minds," he'd said. Because of Arnie, the garden is also a cemetery of buried things, humble roots, treasured relics, and those godawful secrets.

Lila Day watches the bees get drunk on pollen and sunshine. Summer had lingered somewhere else before it came and stayed in Castle River and everything leapt to life all at once. It is downright gaudy. She sighs and lets her eyes close to rest from those daisy riots of July, her ears sharp to the offkey notes of songbirds. She has outlived the age of urgency; she can sit in the shade without a thought of things to be done. Beside her, there is a spent spike of Lupine from last year, and she doesn't care.

Arnie would not approve of the promiscuous propagators left to seed themselves freely, but in the heat of the July garden, Lila knows this: one moment she was a little girl dying to wear makeup and pantyhose and the next she can't see well enough to apply mascara or bend to put a stocking on. All those years they were so young and stupid they didn't even know they were doing it all wrong. Arnie would tell her to let herself have some peace because in the end, all she had were the things she would have done differently. And the end is no place to dwell on all that.

When Lila opens her eyes, the sun is angled, and it ogles her. She wishes Arnie were there to hear about it. Such a habit, babbling to another person about the littlest things. A woman in isolation is a stranger to herself, an unknown creature that can turn on her own heart and mind out of loneliness. Lila thinks that her last day is a good day for turning on herself, turning herself all the way inside out, and coming clean with all that business in the dirt.

Lila and Arnie had worked in the dirt together for so long they traded single gloves, his barely worn left hand for her barely worn right. "Garden gloves for our garden loves." What a quipper! Arnie always said something snappy and sharp. Lila misses that sometimes, hadn't appreciated the blessing of brevity, the simplest staccato string of words.

Lila remembers that Arnie stole the wisteria all those years ago, snipped a cutting to root from the old vine covering the gazebo on the town square. He helped himself to things as if they were put there for his use. They lingered in its shade on their first date and hadn't noticed the sun had slipped past twilight. The lunar world weakened Lila's mind and body. She imagined herself a nocturnal flower, and who knew how lovely a moonflower could be? Arnie knew, that's who. And what was Lila-the-botanist to do with the attention of a floral devotee? She had no choice but to be completely smitten with him. Walking home, their moon shadows chaperoned their steps across the dewy square.

"Grass is overrated," Lila said about her wet feet, and that was enough for Arnie. Before long he was at her door with a shrub in his hand and shrug on his shoulders. It was a *Spirea*—a bridal veil *Spirea*. That was how the man proposed, and how could Lila refuse? A flowering fountain of white blossoms was the perfect path into her heart.

Arnie and Lila married and planted the bridal veil shrub at the edge of the sidewalk where it struggled to thrive. That should have told Lila everything she needed to know about their marriage, but it was not easy for a gardener to give up.

"Gardeners, by definition, are hopeful people," Lila said. "Especially the garden club gals."

The ladies of the All Seasons Garden Club spent the winter months begging Arnie to be their special guest of honor at the annual Spring Splendor Luncheon in March. Arnie took his time before he acquiesced in his practiced humble tone.

"Guess we're going hobnobbing," Arnie told Lila. "I'll be good, if you'll be good."

"I'm always good," Lila said. "I'm only going for the show."

The show was this: those garden club ladies shamelessly gawked at, fawned over, and flirted with Arnie right in front of Lila. It heated her cheeks and dropped her jaw. Arnie, on the other hand, was immune to shame. Unspoken between them all, the fact that one day, sooner than later, all those ladies would be lying naked before Arnie. Thieves are the best actors, blending in as if they led ordinary lives. He turned on the charm and winked aplenty as the women tittered and tipped their teacups, their rheumy eyes crinkled over the floral-patterned rims. Whole lifetimes of practiced modesty completely forgotten when Arnie was near.

"What a lovely brooch, Josephine," Arnie said to the matriarch at the head of the table. "Worthy of wearing to Heaven!"

Lila kept her gaze on the table as Josephine fingered her antique cameo.

"And how many anniversary rings are there on your fingers? Oh, you have earned the right to wear them forever." Hypnotic suggestions rippled off Arnie's tongue into the fragrance above the floral centerpiece. Carnations, the fragrance of funerals and garden club luncheons.

Josephine gave Arnie and Lila their annual invitation to join, and Arnie gave his annual refusal.

"We're just not joiners," Lila explained, surprised at her own mistruth. Arnie's deceptiveness, his habitual lying wore off onto her. They grafted all manner of scions onto waiting root stock, put together large pots of stunning combinations: dark millet and splashy *Coleus* or *Dracaena* spikes and trailing sedums. Lila and Arnie were most definitely joiners.

Arnie Day unapologetically rustled roses. "Stolen roses smell the best," he said. Arnie lied about a lot of things, about people's lives in spoken eulogies, but he never lied about roses. The cabbage roses perfumed the neighborhood with an intoxicating scent of myrrh and musk when they bloomed. Lila's favorite was the climber at the old potting shed. It was the palest pink, the exact color of faded love.

When Arnie was happy with Lila, he used her namesake, *Syringa*, the botanical name for both the French and the Persian lilacs. She was not the first girl wooed by ancient languages, but her botanical name from Arnie's lips was quite the aphrodisiac. It drew her in as if Arnie were Pan and she the nymph named Syringa, who hid herself as a shrub, their private joke because Arnie noticed even the plainest shrub.

When Arnie was angry with Lila, he used the common lilac's species name, *vulgaris*, a name that Lila hated, and this made Arnie's use quite effective. It was true, Lila was common, her face, forgettable and truer to the species than the genus. This was the tension between them, the stress fracture in a porous relationship that threated to deepen into a messy break if they weren't careful.

Arnie loved beauty, he needed beauty like he needed breath. He drooled over orchids and swooned at the scent of *Plumeria*. His penis hardened at the seductive throats of snapdragons and honeysuckle. He dreamed of Georgia O'Keeffe paintings over wallpaper of morning glory vines.

Opposite of Arnie, Lila preferred the simplest daisy, a Shasta or brown-eyed Susan. For all the splash a daisy lacked, they made up for in dependability. Arnie was not dependable. He could not be a person who watched one day be like the day before.

"They have beaten us, these plants," Arnie said in the doorway of the conservatory. "They have out-evolved us." He spread his arms at the lush jungle under glass where he frittered away his time. Lila took that to mean that the plants had designs on Arnie, had made him propagate and tend them. They wanted for nothing but to bloom for the man. It was true, but Lila understood. Arnie's real job, his taxable profession, was dark and literally lifeless.

Arnold Prescott Day hated the title "mortician," as the fourth-generation owner and operator of the Castle River Funeral Home. Castle River was more of a creek from multiple upstream diversions and the drain of suburban life. It was once a trout fisherman's paradise, but Arnie could never sit at the end of a pole when there were flowers to look at and leaves to study. Even as a child, he was a compulsive weeder, pincher, and snipper. His parents were concerned about the boy.

Lila grew up on the other side of the river with a similar uncanny fascination with plants, an overwhelming sense of connection with a separate earthly kingdom. She spent her childhood collecting, pressing, and labeling. Single, perfect specimens were matted and framed beside diplomas from two separate universities. She fashioned herself into a local expert with a vast collection of species. More than once, Lila suspected that Arnie became her husband to share the herbarium. Common property laws. *Vulgaris.*

A plant thief is often a compulsive collector of other things and Arnie accumulated items that pushed against the edges of morality. Lila discovered this after they had married, after they had dreamed the same dream of star gazer lilies and lady bells. For better or for worse. For Lila, discovering Arnie's oddest collection stung and bled. She made it so.

"Don't tell me that dead people are generous, Arnie! It's not like they have a choice." Lila condemned Arnie's practices when she learned that Arnie did not bury everything with the dead bodies in their caskets. He saved all manner of jewelry, rare coins, and priceless heirlooms from that earthen maw.

In the end, it was Lila's own frugal nature that chased away the immediate disgust and secondary revulsion to Arnie's thievery. Waste was something she could not bear. Arnie brought pocket watches, jewelry, medals, and coins and put them into her hands. For this she held his gaze. They had whole conversations with their eyes.

"Stealing from the dead is a victimless crime," Arnie said, and Lila could not argue. She took the things he brought her, put them into jars and buried them in the garden and marked each placement with a distinct poisonous plant, *Datura*, oleander, caster bean, to be certain for her plan. Then she marked the spot on her body, cutting with a sharp grafting knife, her body a keloid map to dangerous botanical alkaloids and buried treasure underneath.

"Another scratch?" Arnie asked with his best concerned funeral director voice. He didn't think she knew about his practiced brow knit, the slight purse of lips. But she knew this and so much more. Syringas were crafty in their subtle ways; lilacs were survivors. Until they were not.

Always, but especially on the garden bench in the heat of July, Lila follows memories and berates herself for not being good at telling which moments in her life were important while they were happening. Turns out they were all important, and this makes Lila laugh out loud. Like plants, they all had something to admire, even common weeds. She loves the intricate venation of horehound leaves, the mathematical spiral of florets that turn into sunflower seeds, the fractal perfection of an everyday bracken fern. She admires the parasitic prowess of Indian paintbrush, the brave defense of cactus, the allure of aubergine belladonna. The poisons were useful for this last day.

While her mind was clear, she went over her end-of-life checklist so she couldn't deceive herself. She'd had enough of deception. The truth was that she fell for a thief, but who had a perfect life? Now that she was old, with eyes as dry as drought, she wants to dream again. About the man who stole plants and precious things, but not her heart. That one is on her; she gave her heart freely.

She noted her body map in a letter to her attorney, posted just that morning. The scarring of her body is more enjoyable than she could admit out loud until just now. It is just a small piece of awful in the grand scheme of things. And since she is coming clean, she admits that she rather likes wearing the marks of Arnie's guilt, rather likes being the map to offer back the buried treasured things.

She drinks the lethal dose and sits next to Arnie's ashes. It doesn't take long.

The Music of the Words

Kurt Luchs

Our mother would recite Yeats,
Frost, Dylan Thomas, and Shakespeare
while doing housework or cooking,
she was a terrible housekeeper
and her cooking was one step removed
from negligent homicide,
but she had a lovely voice
which made the words sing
with a hey nonny nonny
and a permanent case
of postpartum depression.
Sometimes she switched to ballads
made popular among American folkies
by the Clancy Brothers,
Pete Seeger, and Joan Baez.
Either way the music of the words
sunk in deep, the difference between
conversation and verse
was not lost in translation,
the rhythms and rhymes
made it all stick
and we learned that poetry
is simply part of life
like sweeping the floor badly
or burning the toast in tune.

A Tiger's Bite

Ardsheer Ali

Dublin 6. Almost noon. Freezing September day. Blinds drawn. Ticking clock. Ceiling barely visible. Cold lingers around the room. A tiger waiting to pounce on its prey. The heater must still be defunct. I kick away the sheets.

The cold attacks me. I am the prey. It is the fourth day of the grey rain.

I throw open the wardrobe. Drag out a thick sweater. Then another. A beanie. My muffler. The warmest pyjamas I could find at Penneys. The tiger's bite doesn't hurt as much. Maybe I shouldn't sleep naked. But it's the only way I can.

Coffee mug lies beside the sink. Unwashed. Jet of water emerges from tap. Cold. Strong. Breaks down the hardened residue. New beans go in. Followed by boiled water. Drops of milk. A powerful aroma comes out.

I take a sip. My tongue is now burnt.

I go to the balcony. The tiger's teeth dig further into me. But it's almost pleasant. My eyes search the streets. Nobody is around. Only the endless rain. Falling from a grey sky. Splashing in puddles.

I am cursed for my sins. Eternally.

Fifth day. The newspaper is wet. I leave it stretched on the counter. Rain slower. Skies darker. Thunder audible. Lights off. A vibration alerts me. The dining table buzzes. My phone. It's the boss.

He asks how I'm doing.

I'm breathing. Getting by.

Will I be able to do the assignment.

I'm on indefinite leave.

But I'm the only person who can write it.

I sigh.

Please. Soon.

I hum a confirmation. Phone beeps.

Flash of lightning outside. Room turns bright. Then dark again. I switch on the lamplight. Flick the wetness from the paper. Still no news. Boss was right. I'm the only one who can do it.

I climb into bed. The covers are warm. Comfortable. A reek of mildew appears. I urge myself to sleep. It doesn't happen. The clock keeps ticking.

Tick. Tock. Tick. Tock.

Annoying. Frustrating. Infuriating.

I glare at the clock. Pelt my phone. Direct hit. Loud bang. Glass shatters. Satisfaction envelops me. I lose consciousness.

The tiger is there. It crawls towards me. I try to run. But I can't move. It is futile. Remorse is inescapable.

Sixth day. I am preparing spaghetti. Simple food for lonely men. Boiling water runs out the pan. Tesco pasta sauce goes in. Grated cheese as well. A sprinkle of oregano. Salt. A lovely smell.

A plastic fork lies in the cupboard. I dig in. Straight from the pan. A tiger's bite. It is bland. The roof of my mouth is now burnt.

I eat half of the spaghetti. Toss the rest into the bin. And the fork. Pan tops the pile of unwashed utensils. I pull up my jacket's hood. Walk to the balcony door. Step out. Patter echoes all around. A sound appears. Unusual. A mew.

Ginger cat. Skin like a tiger. On the windowsill. Looks at me. Inquisitive gaze. I reach out my hand. It jumps away. Lands on neighbour's balcony. Looks back. Conceited gaze.

Almost evening. Patter grows louder. Sends a jet of piss down my groin. Stops at the tip. I look past the railing. The usual. Nobody around. Pyjamas slide down. Stream of pee rushes out. Goes over the railing. Blends in with the puddles.

Back inside now. Coffee mug in its usual place. Dirty as ever. I clutch the handle. But I can't lift it. Too heavy.

I cannot keep going. I will decay.

On what was supposed to be the seventh day of the grey rain, it stopped. Abruptly, as if Mother Nature had snapped her fingers and declared "That's it." All it left behind was a lingering mist. I woke up before 9 am, made the bed, and heated up the kettle. I threw in some cardamom, cloves, and a slice of ginger. Leaving it on boil, I scrubbed my mug thoroughly until it was sparkling clean. Then I added a dash of milk and sugar in the kettle to prepare the traditional *chai*. It filled the mug up to the brim. I hobbled out to the balcony. The wind was low, weaving around the tufts of my hair. Its crispness settled upon my dry face without becoming bothersome. I drank the tea with gentle sips to prevent my tongue from burning. The fragrance reminded me of home. A memory reel of roadside tea stalls, overcrowded buses, and prickly heat began to play in my mind. I'd have done anything to go back to those days.

I washed the mug and left it upside down on the dining table. In the bedroom, I found the cleanest white shirt in the dresser, ironed out its creases, and pulled its warmth over myself. My only suit hung in the wardrobe, black and forlorn as ever. I dusted it off after putting it on. The blue tie, a gift from an old friend, was already knotted from previous use. It wrapped around my neck with a timid grace. I found my pair of dress shoes beside the dresser and polished them clean. Before strolling out the door, I applied a careless amount of moisturiser on my face.

The little café at the northern end of Rathmines had only a handful of customers when I walked in. I eased into my usual corner armchair and ordered a cinnamon danish. The sun had finally shown up, dissolving the morning mist, dyeing the café in a shade of monochromatic yellow. I peeked through the paper while I ate and, as expected, found nothing of significance. When I left, sprinkles of sugar danced on my tongue and my upper lip carried an aroma of cinnamon. I couldn't recall the last time I'd had anything as satisfying.

Within a couple of minutes, I reached the Portobello harbour. Despite the brisk wind, it was a lovely day with blue skies and generous sunlight. The canal banks were already busy—students, lovers, groups of friends with packs of beers. I crossed the bridge, gazing toward the glimmering waters as I always did. A line of kebab shops appeared on my left; all closed in the early hours. I reached the bus stop at the crossroads and searched for my bus on the screen: it was due to arrive in six minutes.

The 68 arrived after ten minutes. I headed over to the upper deck and slumped into a seat on the left row. The sky turned dark again as the bus went past Inchicore's old houses. Nobody of significance came up the stairs, as I had expected. Some roads were rather serpentine, causing bouts of dizziness, and I closed my eyes many a time. I was safe here. As the bus crossed the Peamount Hospital, I dragged my body off my seat and headed down.

When I alighted, the wind had become strong and irksome. The Newcastle Graveyard was right across the road. A few cars were parked outside its rusted black gates, most of them hatchbacks. It didn't cover a large area from what I could make out. I was there for the first time, and without any signboards, it wasn't easy to find the section I wanted. I dawdled across different rows and columns of graves, as interested (and disinterested) as a teenager scrolling through his social media feed.

At long last, the tombstone I'd been looking for appeared, towering over a mound of sand. A simple grave for a simple man. At its foot, beside a trio of recently-lit incense sticks, lay a fresh bouquet of flowers. I sat down upon my knees. The scent of lavender exuding from the incense wafted into my nostrils and brought back wistful memories. The rough gravel poked through my pants and possibly etched a few scratches on my kneecaps.

"N. Saleem. 1987—2018. A loving husband, a caring father, an incredible man."

Some lines in Arabic followed. They might have been traditional prayers for the dead. To make his grave spacious, to provide him the highest degree of *Jannah*. Or they might have been some kind words about him in Urdu. I'd long forgotten the script. Regardless, I cupped my hands the way I was taught as a child and uttered the few phrases of prayers I still remembered. Tears in my eyes caught me by surprise.

God, have mercy on us all. In this life and the hereafter.

I spread my hands over my face as I hummed *ameen*. In doing so, I wiped away the trail of wetness on my cheeks. The insides of my nostrils had flared up, burning. I realised that I was gasping for air. The blue tie, gifted by this same friend, was choking me with intent to kill. It was only appropriate. In fact, it was poetic.

At that moment, my consciousness was detached from my body. I could no longer recognise my own breathing. My fingers wouldn't obey my will to move them. The coldness of the wind couldn't permeate through my skin, which had become a separate shell in itself. The only thing I could sense was the tiger.

Crouching behind me. Teeth out. Ready to pounce. Running is futile. Tiger is inescapable. I will be mauled to death. In the graveyard. Befitting. A sad demise for a sad person.

It was time to go. But as I was about to close my eyes, a flash of lightning lit up the dark sky.

Thunder roared high above, and down came the grey rain. A cascade of heavy raindrops drenched me in an instant and brought back my consciousness. The tiger was gone. I was able to move again. Clenched my fingers into a fist without effort. Groaning, I pulled myself up, dusted my knees, and headed towards the gates.

By the time I reached home, my heartbeat had slowed down to audible, sporadic *thuds*. Kicking the shoes off my feet, I dug out my laptop from beneath a pile of unwashed clothes on the sofa. Water dripped from my suit and created tiny puddles across the wooden floor. I puffed away the dust from the screen as I opened my inbox. It was cluttered with people trying to sell me stuff I didn't want and colleagues wanting me do their jobs. Only a couple of mails from my boss carried the information I needed. I reviewed these and began to write the article he expected. Or rather, the article I had been fated to write.

TWO ARRESTED IN STABBING OF BANGLADESHI MAN. The Gardaí have arrested two men for the fatal stabbing of an accountant last week. N. Saleem was born in Dhaka, Bangladesh, and had been a resident of Phibsborough for the past four years. He was an associate at a consulting firm in East Wall.

Saleem and his friend were headed home from a restaurant in Drumcondra on Friday night when the storm began. They stumbled upon what is believed to be a drug deal in an alleyway near the DART station. The friend, who wishes to remain unnamed, reported that the men's faces were barely visible but he could make out their identical blue jackets with a tiger emblem on the breast. When they drew their knives out, Saleem tried to defuse the situation but his friend turned and fled, leaving him fending for himself. His dead body was found by the Gardaí half an hour later with multiple stab wounds.

The two suspects were taken into custody earlier this week and currently await trial. They were wearing the same jackets that Saleem's friend identified from the night of the murder. The Gardaí are questioning them to learn more about the others involved in the deal. It is unclear if there had been a racial element to the murder.

Saleem leaves behind his wife and two-year-old daughter. His funeral service took place on Sunday morning at the Newcastle Graveyard. A candlelight vigil in his honour will be carried out on Thursday evening at the Mountjoy Square Park.

Orison

Timmi Sanni

O God, what a monster you've made of life,
this big, bad hand breaking us into shards

as though bodies are glass figurines in the eyes
of a dark universe. In this world, I am a vase

holding up a bouquet of daisies to the heaven
—see, an harvest of beauty in a time wrought

with gore. Once, I was small & beautiful. Now,
I wear fractures on my body, like a new skin.

What is it about life that makes memories
of scars? The function of time as a pendulum

swinging between hurt and joy. I don't know
what is more daunting: struggling between the

fist of a death squeezing too hard—the bird
of hope folding its wings, its hollow bones

crushing as they welcome the uncanny force
of darkness or is it a man chasing after a time

that runs into oblivion & fast? God, do not
feed me to the beasts of the earth. See, I too

am in search of a giant bite of grace at the end
of this hungry road. I am nothing but the calm

of water in a boy's tender palms. Pour me whole
into a canyon. I want to be as tough as the sea.

Color of Want

Travis Stephens

Sea glass was once just trash.
A bottle burst at the surfline
or let slowly sink beyond
the shiny shards scattered like dreams.
Some came back.
This is the taste of ocean, this is
the weight of the wind.
We visited Maine in summer
& I sought beach glass like jewels.
You watched for shells;
sand dollars, whelks, helmets of cockles.
They filled a tissue bed shoebox.

At home the glass filled
bottles and mason jars set
on a window's wide sill.
Dust lessens a shine.
You made pen & ink drawings
of a shell, a chiton slipper,
kelp's careless wave.

An errant sunbeam enters
this room & it too ignores
the papers on the desk.
No, I won't sign today.

There are empty shoeboxes
in the trash & savage
wire hangers want to be clothed.
Beer bottle browns & Coke blues;
tincture of memory,
the colors of want.

Eugenia

Mirela Hristova

He jumped up in front of her like an ugly giant. His unusual height, his broad shoulders, his repulsive pockmarked face. He was saying something urgent, making exaggerated gestures in the air. And he was smiling.

"Eimai xeny," she said. That was one of the few Greek phrases she had managed to learn in the two weeks since her arrival in Athens. *I am a foreigner.*

At 24, she had just survived her fiancé's death. In the months and years to come, she would often reflect upon the whim of ancient gods to spare her life. The Iron Curtain had just fallen, they had both been of the "right" origin, superbly educated, ex-socialist *nomenklatura*. And then he was killed.

Money—and power—had to change owners.

Now here she was, in the hot, unbearably humid July afternoon, in this affluent central area. Of all places in the world, Greece had been the only option for her to flee to. Penniless, alone, and scared, her whole creature cried *Foreign.*

But the man in front of her kept talking and smiling.

Obviously, he wanted to know her name. "Alekos," he said pointing to himself, in the universal language of gestures, with an endearing boyish simplicity. Just like in kindergarten.

She smiled. How lovely it felt, for once, to be a child again, to forget everything—the impossible past, her unfulfilled future, her University degrees, all the other languages she spoke. Foreign.

"Eugenia," she said, and, fragile and trembling, she ran away in her pink girlish dress.

In the following days, she changed her route. Office—Language school—Rented flat. Those were the vertices of her new triangular world, defined by the international project she had miraculously won just before leaving her country. She deliberately chose different streets, alternative hours for her solitary walks, just to make sure she would not accidentally bump into the huge figure, the only person she knew in this foreign town.

After a week or so, she went to a remote district. The Archaeological Museum was somewhere here, according to her map. "Free entrance," the small letters on the back read. She had been a youth champion in orienteering, but somehow that did not help when she got lost.

Her name, though, did.

Eugenia. She learned in her Modern Greek class that it meant *nobility, kindness.* It served like a magic weapon that triggered open, friendly smiles on people's faces whenever she said it. There was a hidden meaning, a deeper symbol behind the everyday surface of this foreign world. Exploring this ancient labyrinth where myths and gods and Vespas and Japanese tourists in shorts mingled in a slightly distorted version of time was frightening and tempting at the same time. *Relax,* her inner voice said. *Relax, there is nothing more to lose.*

"Eugenia." The voice came from behind, her name sounding strange, as if addressed to a different person.

How was it possible? There were three million citizens and more, not counting the tourists who flooded the city like lazy, perspiring flies under the scorching sun's heat. While she was still considering whether to turn and face the giant man, a chorus of voices repeated: "Eugenia, Eugenia, Eugenia."

Sure. It wouldn't be a Greek tragedy without a chorus, she thought.

Slowly, she turned. There, in front of her, were a dozen young men and women, relaxed and friendly, and smiling.

"He said you must be an actress," a man said in English. "Beautiful."

"Singer?" another one said.

"Eimai xeny," she mumbled, her eyes bewildered and wild. She needed an escape.

"Eugenia, come, come, Eugenia," shouted the young girls.

And here he was, huge, tall, his arms opened wide, and before she could react, he embraced her in a giant hug, as if they had known each other for ages. Ages ran in a different mode here, she had already learned.

"We go for lunch, *paraia, group,"* someone said. "You come with us." This was not a question. They carried her along.

They managed a small family company, later one of the men, Alekos's brother, explained, and "the boys and the girls," he gestured towards the smiling, chatty group, worked for them. "They are so nice and they work hard for us," he said. "Taking them to lunch now and then is a minor treat we can offer."

The boys and the girls were enjoying their food. Every dish looked like a picture from a cookbook. Never had Eugenia seen a whole restaurant menu on one table. *One must enjoy every single moment. To live means to be happy*, their gleaming faces said. Thankfully, they did not ask many questions.

She learned that they had been just in front of the brothers' office when she passed on her way, looking for the Archaeological Museum.

From that day on, she was not alone. She had found friends, *paraia,* group, family. Or, rather, the group had found her.

She no longer said, "*Eimai xeny,*" after that first lunch with them.

"Yes, you are *xeny*, foreign, but we are friends, *filoi*," Alekos's brother said in half-English, half-Greek.

The Greek word for hospitality, *philoxenia*, is derived from those two words and it means *to love, be friendly with the foreign*. That was one of her newly acquired practical lessons he taught her. She already loved this new school.

Alekos had never been one for school. He never made a point of learning any foreign language, which is a crime, with so many tourists coming to Greece. "It is a surprise how such a lazy, stupid man makes friends with so many people—and beautiful women—in the street," his brother often joked.

Alekos didn't say anything. He only smiled.

Strange, she thought, from time to time, *where have his pockmarks gone*? Still there, but had she gone blind? Smiling, comforting eyes—that was what she saw. She was not alone anymore.

They were curious about her, but not excessively. Some of the things she said in her limited broken Greek, mixed with several other languages, were too strange, too complicated, too surrealistic to be true. *Perhaps, it was just the language barrier*, they thought. She was here with them, she was one of them now, and that seemed to be enough. They took her for what she was. She relaxed.

More and more new people came in following months. *How was it possible?* she wondered occasionally. *Three million citizens and more, not to count the tourists, and Alekos makes a point of making friends with almost all?* And it happened so easily, so nonchalantly. He just shrugged and smiled, accepting it with a sincere childish gratitude, as if making all those friends was a lifelong gift to him. It made her think. It humbled her.

"You should consider becoming a politician," she told him one day, when her Greek had improved.

"No need," he answered simply, "when we have friends." He smiled.

That was another lesson she learned from him. When some of those numerous friends became too insistent, too curious about her past, she kept silent. *Silence is gold,* her Granny had always said, back in her old life. *Especially when you smile.*

It was high time she practised it.

Usually, that worked. People were fooled. They took her for what she looked like—a young, beautiful woman. Yet another of Alekos's "discoveries." She didn't speak. She might be stupid—or intelligent—they didn't care. All of them, except for Alekos. Very, very rarely, when she least expected it, he would look at her when someone new was pressing her for answers. Half-jokingly, half-seriously, he would say, "Leave her alone. She is a *kataskopos.*"

Later in her rented flat, she looked the word up in the dictionary. *A spy,* it read.

Days and weeks, and months went on. She settled into her new life. She gained several kilos. She began to dress like them, look like them, speak their language, enjoy life and food like them. Live like them to the fullest. The heat and humidity no longer oppressed her.

She no longer slept. How could one possibly sleep under this magic Athens sky, where stars and Gods were so close and so alluring, and the night was so inviting, humming with the distant roar of Vespas, headed for the sea? The smell of sea was everywhere, permeated by the scent of love. There were mermaids on the shore.

In the early morning hours she came back home from midnight walks to the nearby hills, where, her new friends had said, ancient gods lived. Exhausted, she slept for an hour or so, took a shower, and got ready for the new work day like everybody else. It was such a relief. The photograph of her killed fiancé was still there by her bed, but she didn't sleep with it anymore. How could she if she didn't sleep at all?

She didn't cry. If you keep yourself busy with people and life, you won't have the time to cry. Is it possible to forget?

She had told Alekos, and everybody else, that her name was Eugenia. She had almost believed it. She had almost forgotten that it was the name the Secret Services had chosen for her. They hadn't asked her if she wanted it, or not.

To her surprise, she did.

Poetry First Prize

If Betelgeuse Explodes, I Will Be Sad

Shana Ross

The twelfth brightest star fell to twentieth and don't worry,
most people say, the arc of the cosmos is long and bends.
The world has never ended before, so we will survive this too.

We trust the stars, steer by them. Name your cat Astrolabe, the grey one,
then use an app that will take you from here to there,
recalculating, recalculating at every wrong turn, indefatigable.

I love the stars because they flicker. I love the stars because they recede.
I love the stars because they trace perfect circles if you plant yourself
on a hill and let the aperture stay open all night, exposed.

We call this constancy. It took us a thousand years to unearth
pottery painted with the explosion of a star that could be seen
in daylight, that came and went so long ago the stories too

began, crested, left us. The waters of time are no tide, they
twist and flow and gnaw the earth, riverine. Don't apologize
for stuffing joy into your cheeks one acorn at a time. Eat. Eat.

Don't worry, they say, these are cycles that history will see clearly.
When you live in too much light you cannot see the stars
yet they exist. After a snow, the stars alone can reflect

just enough to see the trees when the new moon has nothing but
shadow to show us. We wait. We gaze into promises and old maps.
Binary breadcrumbs, beaming from satellites; the not quite

stars we made to surround us, obey us, guide us so we never
have to rely on magnetism, the kind that points us, listing, to the poles.
We look to constellations for other things now. I love the stars because

when you look at them, the twinkle you see is combustion long past,
lightyears between what they know and what you've just learned.
Don't worry, they say, we can still make predictions from precedent.

I had a bike that worked until it broke, stressed metal shearing irreparably.
I had an aunt who recovered from everything, until she died at 98.
I love the stars because I want to believe their wandering tugs

at our fate, bears responsibility for the pointing of warships across seas,
the aiming of people into entanglements, all bounce and bruising ricochet,
ripping from roots, falling spent, staying down. This is the shame

of the hunter, the temptation to fade. In the history of the universe,
there is no overlap between those who fall on their swords for honor
and the long list of people who deserve to be run through. Don't worry.

This will be the most toothsome grief: the winking out of one
light in all the heavens that had a name sweet as wild blueberries
& could be recognized as quick as first love in a full sky.

Box

Mandira Pattnaik

In order to defy the seemingly immovable order of things, the twelve-year-old boy will not only begin to think "out of the box" but will also imagine there's no such box: no applause ringing in his ears, no surge of voices from the undulating valley as far as he can see, no march toward the periphery.

He'll pretend to be a professional chef. Sometimes a certified tea-brewer. Practice making a proper cup of tea. As though the camera is rolling, he'll go down to every bit of detail: how to add extra steps to strengthen the brew, temperature of the kettle, whether to use double-filtered water. He'll stretch his voice to almost a drawl when interrupting instructions to share, oh-so-little anecdotes about childhood in Kashmir, about an imaginary girlfriend from Pehelgaum

He'll argue whole-leaf-tea-versus-loose-tea with his dad, while tending to their apple orchard and his father will look at the slopes, teal and exquisite like Monet's landscape, and not speak further when the boy says Black Tea needs four or five minutes and Oolong only three. His dad will examine the boundary of his orchard, the steep drop on the western side where someone as imaginative as his son flung herself because her beliefs were out of the box—rested on the wheels of fortune. The boy's mother was convinced she'd be reincarnated as royalty, live in the mahogany-and-glass castle up in the mountains, a tiny kitchenette all to herself just where she'd make pies for the king.

A sigh later, his dad will retire to their modest dwellings.

The boy will fix broken limbs growing inward toward the trunks of trees. Later, he'll seal the cut made off-flush to the parent branch, speculate whether the festering wound underneath will ever heal.

He'll look at his hands, same as mum's. Think of the juicy apple marmalade his mum used to make, her delicate hands as she spread it on warm chapatis. He'd wonder the outcome if apples were first treated with vinegar before being boiled. Will he name the new marmalade recipe something so exotic audiences will latch onto it, because they won't be able to translate it?

In the evening, he'll sit before the TV. View the box before he switches it on. A window. The shape, rigid and unwelcoming. With lines and edges he's trying to defy, fly away to spaces outside, spaces not for him.

He'll find himself away, far away, as long as the culinary show runs.

Later, the boy will write to people he thinks can help him. Names scribbled on a piece of paper when end credits roll.

His father, one particular evening, will be mumbling minutes before the event—the event in which he will throw the boy out of the box he's currently in.

Unable any longer to bear the tapestry his son has been weaving, Dad will thrash the boy till his palms bleed. The twelve-year-old won't be able to finish the sudden outlandish story he's been telling Dad, where the perfectly coated minced meat recipe has been stolen from one of the Mahelinese tribal families residing in the far east, and which may be retrieved if they be allowed to raid the Nihutise.

That'll be the night the boy will post a note on the wall behind the stove, and under a lonely moon, take a detour through the dirt path that bifurcates the orchard, giving himself a few moments when he passes the steep western side.

The 5:45 morning bus will be the one he'll take, stopping by the barn just as an afterthought.

Once inside the bus, he'll survey the passengers' faces, boarding and de-boarding, in the dim light of pre-dawn. The 5:45 will snake down the curve of the hill, climb onto the next and next. Most will not bother about the boy travelling alone, but the butcher will recognize him.

"Where to?" he'll ask. The boy will cook up a story about an ill grandmother.

"Never had a Granma, did you? She lived across the border, been dead long, no?"

"Sorry, she's—she's—an aunt, mother's third sister. Fractured hips."

"Oh, I see. But where's your father?"

"Home. Old enough to go alone!"

"Sure!"

He'll roll his eyes, grumble about something, get off at the next stop.

The bus will leave the perches of the hills, slither into the plains where the district town the boy has never been before will have just woken up. At a bustling eatery, he'll get off with the others, trailing one particular family with three howling toddlers, follow them inside, and thinking he is part of the family, be served buns with thick red chutney. Later, with the family denying any relation to him, and no money on him, he'll be washing dirty dishes piled around an even dirtier water spout.

His father meanwhile will scour the length and breadth of the orchard, returning ever so frequently to peer at the steep side one more time just to make sure. By noon, he'll discover the note on the kitchen wall, drop on all fours and cry himself hoarse.

The boy will spend the next six-quarter years washing dishes, during which he'll be thrashed and brutalized for suggesting tweaking this recipe or that on the menu. Learning life's hard lessons, for two square meals a day, he'll keep himself confined to the water spout and its square sink. His dreams will turn brittle, waiting for a last shovel of earth to bury them good.

One of the days, with a sore wound on his knee, he'll limp to the customer in thick glasses, dark maroon rucksack, browsing the menu card. The boy will recognize him—chef-anchor he's seen on TV. He'll tell him so, his infinite admiration, expect the tide to turn. They'll talk, they'll giggle, to the envy of the other waiter boys. The boy will look excited like they've never seen him before.

The man will pay a little tidy cash to the owner who'll let the boy go with him.

An orange autumn afternoon many moons later, the boy will slice tomatoes thin, place them in one of six identical pristine-white porcelain bowls while the crew sets up cameras and lighting. He'll fill other bowls with cardamom pods, garlic, ginger, dried shrimps, ground tamarind paste. See to it that the table is placed in the middle of an apple orchard for that rustic, authentic appeal. He'll arrange the polished wok on the stove, ready to be lit, and larders and spoons to the right of the oven. On the side of the bowls will be bright green lettuce leaves for that perfect color contrast.

When the chef-anchor-from-TV arrives to take his position at the table and the camera begins to roll, he will swiftly retire to somewhere outside the square camera-frame and think of the steely box with stiff edges and corners that'll not let anyone defy it. The tight box in life nobody escapes out of.

The story

Matthew Dettmer

A man comes to the ICU coughing blood from tumors that fill the canals of his lungs like factories dumping death into rivers now his cough is getting tired and blood is sitting in those canals blocking oxygen from making its way down them right now we can blast enough air through a mask but we won't be able to for long his wife lunges down the hall hits the buzzer for entrance and I let her know it'll be a few minutes she looks at me like I've pulled one of her teeth with pliers I go through the story with the team outside the room the CT scan the oncologist's notes the unanswered questions about hospice I walk to his bed see him stroke his wife's cheek saying "hey little girl" with crusted blood on his lips and usually I have to say "death" out loud but not this time because it's starting to hover in the air between the two of them as they squint through trying to see each other as it thickens.

Virtual Season 2020

Helen Bournas-Ney

Visor down and at a slant, a Magritte sky
above me, I linger lakeside (that is . . .
by a puddle, on a retro sky-blue lawn
chair in our parking lot). It's all—a lot,
to keep on moving that confounded chair
to here, there, everywhere that sun allows,
all afternoon it's moving, with the news,
the shadows, and a broken asphalt masked
with leaves. We hope this day impervious
to truant winds. We keep on moving toward
the light—that somehow always leaves,
and even when it's there, feels so uncertain.
Is it the sun? Is it the light that's bouncing
off the Hudson Yards behemoths?—so hard
sometimes to tell the sun
                                        from shimmer.
The day, the month, the ground itself somehow
escapes us. I keep on trying just to make it
small: to figure out just where to put my chair.
I think it must be anywhere that sun allows.

Of Porridge, Untethered Things, and Rabbits

Somto Ihezue Onyedikachi

The boy is taken with the forest, the rains, how they once collected in the trees, tapering down on his skin in beaded drops. The musk of wet bark, bold, consuming. And there's the sunlight, gold mist stealing through the canopy. When the forest breaks day with its many songs, its chirps, and croaks, it calls to him, like music longing to be heard. On the roots of the gmelinas, the boy picks mushrooms. He knows to stay clear of the dapperlings, their red sprouts, a bright toxic scream. Over the roots and through the low-hanging branches, the boy pours out onto the bank of a babbling spring. At the water's edge, peppers, scent leaves, and pumpkins grow in the most intentional patterns, their sweetness dampening the air. The boy nips the pumpkin leaves, gnawing on one and stashing the rest into his raffia bag.

"How do we know which leaves to eat?" the boy once asked his grandmama.

"Whatever the antelopes eat, so can we."

"Even the grass?"

"Well, not everything," she had laughed.

In the boy's village, the New Yam Festivals were held as the rains poured their last. Under a full moon, the farmers would haul their first yams–some bulkier than grown men–into the village square. To ancestors past, they'd offer the yams in gratitude. Encircling a large fire, the elders would roast their tubers, and eat them with salted palm oil, oil beans, and ùtàzì leaves. Like drums of war, pestles would be heard for miles as boiled yams got pounded in mortars. With bitter-leaf soup, the meshed yam would be swallowed in small folds.

But this time, the year rolled out and the rains did not come. With the soil cracking under the heat, the villagers harvested what little they could before the scorching sun consumed everything. The boy's cousin, Nene, the one at the university up in the city, had said something about a layer in the sky, how it was waning, destroyed by smoke and fumes, how it caused the drought.

"Bear Nene no mind," the boy's grandmama had told him. "Our ancestors have held back the rain, for many have strayed from them."

Like every other family, the boy and his grandmama had to celebrate the New Yam Festival in their home. There was no gathering, no pounding, no large fires.

"We should make porridge yam," the grandmama suggested.

"Porridge yam?"

"Yes, it'd go perfectly with some roast rabbit."

The boy half nodded.

"Run along now, go get me some vegetables," she nudged him. "And check the traps!" she added as he ran off.

Porridge yam and roast rabbit, this is why the boy is nipping pumpkin leaves by the spring. The spring had endured despite the drought, its water a shimmer in the dark. With all its shadows, the forest does not frighten the boy. His parents, hunters, had lived at its skirts. They'd come home dragging giant antlered deers, wild boar, and baskets of fish. They taught him to tie a knot, and to set traps. One day, they went into the forest and never came out.

Done plucking the vegetables, the boy wanders off, farther into the woods. He comes upon a heap of dry grass and scatters it to reveal a cage trap. Inside, a rabbit like a white cloud shivers. He draws the blade his father had carved him and his father's voice steals into his mind, *do not hesitate.*

The boy skips home. He stops to chase a rooster before hurrying back on. Home, he finds his grandmama crushing palm kernels. He kneels and kisses her cheek. She smells of old wood and charcoal. She looks into his raffia bag, and displeasure sets on her face.

"No rabbits?"

"Yes." The boy bites his fingers. "I think they've all left our village."

"And where did they go?"

"I–I don't know."

"We'll have to make do," she says, handing him a tiny yam tuber. The yams are all tiny, the drought had made sure of it. The boy dices it into the pot of water sitting on the fireplace. While his grandmama chops the pumpkin leaves, the boy goes to grind the peppers and mushrooms. As the yams soften, she calls him to pour in the palm oil.

"Careful now," she says, as he tilts the oil into the pot. She always lets him run such little errands around the kitchen, except with the soup. "You'll ruin it," she always says whenever he asks to help.

"Do I have to be a hunter?" The boy asks, pouring the oil.

"Yes, just like your father and mother." His grandmama stirs as he pours,

"You come from an old line of hunters."

"I don't know if I want to be one."

Ladle in her hand, his grandmama stops. "So what will you be?" She swipes the ladle with a finger and tastes the porridge.

"I could go to the university." The boy sets down the oil keg and returns to the grinding stone. "Cousin Nene said I could learn to be a– a–" He fumbles for the word, squinting, as he scratches his neck. "A chef!" He bursts out. "She said I could cook in the city, and get something called a five star and—"

"I told you to stop listening to Nene," his grandmama cuts in. "A boy can't be a—" She looks down at him and pauses. Back and forth with the grinding stone, his hands move in a knowing manner. The grinding slab tilts to the side, but the boy doesn't stop, he knows it will steady.

"A boy can't be a what, grandmama?"

She does not answer. She slides the chopped vegetables into the pot. The boy comes up behind her, and before she can stop him, he takes the ladle and stirs. His grandmama watches him, his hands, how they move, on a journey, like a stream.

"Perhaps you could make the soup for dinner."

The boy stops to stare at her. "Are you sure?" He asks with narrowed eyes. "I wouldn't want to ruin it."

"You won't."

Like the flames from the fireplace, the boy beams.

"That's enough." The grandmother takes the ladle from him. "Off you go, go see if that trap of yours has caught a rabbit or something."

She watches the boy speed out the house, certain he won't return, not with a rabbit.

Morendo

musical term indicating a decrease in volume or tempo

Claire Scott

I am having trouble memorizing you
once I memorized entire passages from *The Waste Land*
    April is the cruelest month, breeding
    Lilacs out of the dead land
but I am having trouble memorizing you
as you move more slowly, more softly
unfinished sentences, words left hanging
and I forget what they were, what you
were wearing, what we ate for lunch
was it a cheese omelette or leftover stew

I found a wizened peach in the cupboard
behind our pills, did you put it there? did I?
Aricept, Atenolol, Coumadin, Lunesta, Neurontin, Xanax
an alphabet of pharmacological miracles
to keep your heart beating, to keep our minds limber
do you know I sneak *Lunesta* the nights I sleep
sleepless beside you, asking for *more time, please more time*
my prayers landing wide of the mark, it's been too long,
god has given up and moved to greener pastures

Muted days with occasional staccato bursts
    a grandson's graduation
    a poem published in *AARP*
then once more a *diminuendo*, a *ritardando*
softer and slower, the tempo of *grave*
until you are barely a whisper
like a Luna moth at dusk
flickering in the lamplight
or a pale heart that has had enough

Leaving me bruised and bewildered, but still standing
rising from the shroud of sleep
into the haze of secondhand days
moving listlessly, little memory left
sometimes I forget I am alive
but the coffee smells fresh this April morning
the finches are singing high C's
and dull roots are stirring with spring rain
shantih   shantih   shantih

Bad city girl in the back of the bus with headphones on, 42 minutes after taking an edible

Selena Cotte

Men you ruin a good thing when I can hear you smack your lips
my fall apart wrap dress readjusted
as I toggle disgust and guilt:
Who knew it was a windy day?
Some moral woman would tell me
I know how to have found out.
And call me easy, but that's it for me:
I'm mildly crying about the necessity of spring
and that no one will know anything
they won't let themselves see.

I'm always learning things the hard way
pushing buttons that say **DO NOT PRESS**
abusing our safe word *(raspberry)*
by laughing when you stopped.
Yet when I admit I'm afraid of success
that's narcissism too.

I pass the Chicago Cannabis Alliance
close to the dispensary line out the door.
Guess who runs these streets,
prettier blondes in casual shorts.
I feel overdressed and out of place
like a bunny or something scared.
When I walked out the door
red eyes, flapping skirt
you turned away and asked if I'm carrying my mace.

It took a few years, but I finally want to leave Chicago.
Getting off the bus in Andersonville
I scared a man in front of the feminist bookshop,
dismissing his stuttering as harassment.
Who can't speak, now? Punk.
But it was really just a hand wave and a walk past.

The store is at capacity, he was trying to say
or so the shopkeeper inside let me know.
I didn't even wait to enter
walking away with a sickness
the fog spreading out from within.

It's just all too easy these days
and I've been getting way too intimate
with the thrill.

Cooking Alone

Sandra Kolankiewicz

But once I was finished, I had no one
to split it with. Imagine the best news

you receive with no body to relate
to, that the letter arrives without eyes

to read with you, the highest honor
awarded, not one soul to confide your

secret pride. Sharing is everything but
for when you desire solitude, not the

same as wanting to be alone. I had
to show my fine lunch to the birds who hid

from the cat, compelled to announce my luck
to the bare trees and the open sky, a

plane passing so high overhead as to
be invisible, promoting itself

but still impossible to find, all those
strangers traveling somewhere together.

Danielle's Balloons

Dutch Simmons

Passing the bio bags didn't bother me. Bio bags were used to collect human remains and given to coroners tasked with getting DNA samples to identify the dead. We had dozens of body bags that were of no use; the largest identifiable piece I found was part of a foot in a well-polished Gucci loafer.

The smell haunted me. The acrid, burning plastic-soaked in gasoline stench, permeated our paper ventilators. Flashbacks to my youth and army battles with plastic soldiers whose untimely demise was via "flamethrower"—a can of my mother's hairspray and a lighter.

It was ridiculous to say the air carried the stench of death. Sense of smell was illusory at best at Ground Zero, which had become Hell on Earth. Smoldering ash, consisting of concrete and steel, hissed and smoked. Pockets of fires lapped at our legs as we walked the banks of the River Styx searching for souls buried in the mud. We found a few remnants of humanity in the mundane; torn business cards, melted name tags, and cracked desktop picture frames with blackened photos.

The heat was suffocating. When you removed your mask gasping like a fish out of water, you absorbed a lung searing liquid-fire chemical elixir. Tears weren't shed in protest; they had been expended days prior.

As a former search and rescue climber, I was assigned to a hastily formed team consisting of policemen, firemen, and steelworkers. My day job in finance disappeared along with my firm in the Second Tower. Divine Intervention kept me out of the office on the morning of the 11th. As a result, I did God's work solving a biological puzzle consisting of pieces of the dead in order to bring bereaved loved ones closure.

Fueled on an endless supply of Red Cross coffee and gallows humor borne from an omnipresent fear of mortality, the dogs helped me get through the day.

Rescue dogs were as professional as anyone else working in Hell. Probably more so. It took a week before they got protective paw booties. I had cut or burned through several pairs of gloves; my boots begged for mercy. Dogs with longer coats were patted down and doused with water when they smoldered. They never whined or barked in complaint. They were our equals; they were our superiors.

An obscene amount of food arrived. New York City had become Jewish grandmothers overnight. Guilt and suffering were assuaged through endless meals. Every chain and family-owned restaurant delivered to Ground Zero, an embarrassment of riches given every restaurant for several blocks had disappeared into the ether.

Supply ships on the Hudson delivered industrial dog food bags. When they saw the 100-pound bags being carried, the dogs circled and yipped like excited puppies. Twice a day we watched their metamorphosis: co-worker to puppy, and back.

We created makeshift dining tables out of piles of debris. Conversations were stilted; locker room humor prevailed.

A box of exquisitely wrapped sandwiches with shimmering gold foil caught the attention of some of the guys. Like seeing a lightning bug out of season; it registered and disappeared.

I recognized the "DB" monogram on the foil. I knew who made them.

Greedily, we unwrapped sandwiches, devoured the food like locusts descending upon a field. One ironworker eyed his sandwich warily. I called him "Fritz" because of the ring of German Iron Crosses around his neck. Tattoos like that garnered attention.

"Take your time," I offered. "Please savor it."

He eyed me and the sandwich with suspicion, but grabbed a second after his first bite.

"It's focaccia," I explained. "With *pâté*, and pear jelly. It's from Daniel Boulud."

The name drop of one of the most famous chefs in the world went unacknowledged.

Sandwiches were chased with black coffee. I longed for a glass of sauterne and ached to lie back and stare at a flawless blue sky. I wanted my former life back.

As we geared up, Fritz turned to me.

"We should go to Danielle's Balloons when this is over."

Five years later, I walked down Madison Avenue with three colleagues. Search and rescue work remained on hold as I resumed my position in the "real world."

We discussed the markets on our way to happy hour as three massive ironworkers approached in our direction. Toxic masculinity surged; neither group cared to give way.

A tell-tale trail of Iron Crosses peeked out from above the shirt collar on the lead ironworker.

My colleagues bailed on the game of chicken while I deliberately bumped Fritz. His coworkers were wide-eyed in disbelief; the balls of the "suit!"

An ass-kicking was not part of the 2-for-1 happy hour, and my colleagues disapproved of my getting in Fritz's face.

"Clench your fists and I'm telling your pals how much you love dainty sandwiches and wanted me to take you to Danielle's Balloons," I hissed.

The words were gravediggers unearthing long buried memories as Fritz searched me in recognition, before absorbing me in a massive bear hug.

"Let's drink," I gasped as he crushed the life out of me.

Monkey Bar was around the corner. The place startled at the odd bed-fellows bellying up to the bar, eventually taking it over.

We drank with a vengeance.

Fritz and I shared snippets of stories to our respective groups but mostly kept it to ourselves. It was our moment.

We drank to remember and drank even more to forget.

For the first time in five years, I was home.

We never made it to Danielle's Balloons.

Warning

Carolyn Martin

When confronted with the limits of the known world,
a 16th-century European cartographer inscribed the warning
"Here Be Dragons" on a small copper globe. Beware: What lies
beyond is unexplored—and perilous.
—Jodi Cobb, "Strange Reflections,"
National Geographic, March 2019

First you need   a mountain   even a mesa
butte   bluff   or high-rise balcony   will do
any height   to widen   your view   of oceans
forests   canyons   streams   car-clogged arteries
joggers   pacing past   mothers strolling
strollers down   leafy suburban streets
Then find   the edge   where the sky melts   into
topography   and wait   for flames   four legs
a scaly frame   Listen for   roars muting
seagull screams   screeching cars   or voices
quarreling   beyond   your backyard fence
Conjure up   St. George   to ward off   your fear
Listen and wait   How long   is up to you
If they don't   appear   ease yourself   down
into the world-at-hand   Begin to forage   through
cracks   and chinks   and crevices   through slits
and splits   and rifts   Be aware   unknowns
find   a way   of sneaking through   like love
and loss   grief and regret   prejudice and hate
Beware of perils   lurking nearby   Investigate

Cúpla Focal

Máiréad Hurley

"Do you remember going with your Grandad?"

His son's small body was being rattled so violently, it was hard to tell if his nodding was a response to the question or the road. The truck's cab had once been their confessional, but its engine was getting louder with age, and the boy was getting quieter.

"I think so."

Seán had bought the truck soon after they arrived in America. There was no real need for it: he was never much of an outdoorsman and had only fully filled the bed once, helping a friend move, but he had been desperate to own one for as long as he could remember.

When Adam was younger, Seán would lift him the enormous distance from the ground to the front passenger seat and take him to the park, or the movies, or just out for a drive. They were in the truck the first time Adam mentioned liking a girl; it was where Seán told him stories of home and introduced him to his favourite bands. His CDs were still in the glove compartment, but the player had broken last year.

"On the River Ilen. He only took you once, you were very small," Seán said, trying to jog his memory while atoning for the lack of it, "but you'll have to show me the ropes," he smiled, "because he never took me at all."

Seán's father had seen fishing as a solitary activity, and Seán considered it a great honour when he offered to take his grandson. It was only recently that Seán realised how different his own childhood was to Adam's, and he wasn't sure if he was resentful of that, or if Adam was, or if he was imagining things.

"But you do know what you're doing."

Seán wasn't sure if this was a question. He had been reading and watching YouTube videos about fishing for a couple of weeks. He knew he was a little out of his depth, but this still seemed like something they should do. Men fish. All over the world, men fish and they get to know each other again and find space to talk. Adam was twelve now, the truck wasn't enough anymore, but it could take them there.

They rumbled past strip malls and billboards advertising food and faith and financial services. They cleared the main highways and drove deeper into the country. Seán hadn't bought the GPS. He took a left turn he felt reasonably sure of, silently cursing the rising sun, hoping it wouldn't matter too much if they arrived late, hoping more that his son wouldn't know they were lost, or at least wouldn't say anything if he did.

The sun was just about to climb above them when Seán saw the sign he was looking for: Abbott Lake. Relieved, he followed the dirt road to the car park.

It was just the two of them. Seán had expected there to be others out today, and though he worried that they knew something he didn't—wrong time? season? place?—he was pleased it was quiet. He showed Adam how to hook the bait and how to throw the line. He was impressed with his boy's arm and told him so. Adam smiled shyly.

They sat on the bank, holding their rods, and looking out across the lake. It was perfectly still even around their lines, which sliced the water's surface with diagonal incisions but left it otherwise undisturbed. Seán wondered what was going on underneath, whether the unseen world was alive and busy and filled with creatures eating and struggling and breeding and evolving. Did they sense the intrusion of the cord? Were they tricked by the bait?

Seán felt like he was acting, playing the role of a father in a movie. He resisted the urge to say, "So how's school?" and let Adam speak first, let himself be comfortable when they were quiet. He completely relaxed after a while. They talked naturally and joked around. He took a beer from the cooler and let Adam try a sip.

The sun was at its highest point, and Seán was nodding off when Adam sat up with a start. "Dad." The rod shook in his hands. He leapt to his feet. "Dad!" Seán jumped up too and threw his own rod down.

"Christ, have you got one?"

"What do I do?" Adam asked, panicked, wrestling with the rod, his eyes locked on where the water was frothing and splashing.

"Oh my God you've got one! Reel it in! Hold on tight!"

"I can't let go!"

"What do you mean let go? Don't let go! Reel it in!" Seán thought he saw a tail, and he nearly jumped in the air with excitement.

"I can't hold it with just one hand!"

Seán understood the dilemma and gripped the rod with both hands above Adam's. "Now?" the boy asked.

"Now! I've got it."

Adam tentatively took his right hand off the pole. It stayed in place. Seán wasn't going to let it move an inch. The boy took the reel and turned it quickly, feeling more and more resistance, the line becoming so taut that he worried it might snap. Concentrating, trusting his father's grip, he took his left hand off the rod too and used all the strength of both arms to turn the handle.

"It's coming," Adam shouted, "we've got it!" The line shot out of the water, whipping their catch up into the air and towards them. It landed, a long, grey creature flopping on the bank. Adam ran towards it. "Look!" he laughed. "Look, Dad, we got it!" Seán could have cried with pride and exhaustion.

Panting, Adam examined their fish. Its eyes were wide, and it jumped around fiercely. The hook protruded through its scaled face. Smiling, he looked back at his dad, "What now?"

Seán paused. He hadn't thought about this part. "Well, we should . . ."

"Throw it back?"

"Yep. Yeah, we should."

"Or keep it?"

He looked at his son. Of course they should keep it. That's what you do with a fish you've caught. It probably wouldn't survive if they threw it back in, anyway. They grinned at each other. "Yeah. We'll keep it. Definitely."

"We could have it for dinner?"

"Great idea." He didn't know how to prepare a fish, but Adam looked so excited. "Dinner it is."

"How do we kill it?"

He had no idea. He imagined cutting its head with a knife or bashing it with a rock. He didn't have a knife and didn't want to smash it. He looked at it flapping about and tried to think. It wasn't slowing down. His son looked up at him, smiling expectantly.

"Look," he hoped he sounded confident, "they can't breathe out of the water. Grab the icebox. We'll just put it in and it'll be dead before we get back."

Seán leant over it, wondering if he was being cruel. It glistened as it leapt around, scales turning blue in the sunlight. "Thank you," he whispered.

Adam returned with the icebox.

"Do you want to?" Seán asked him.

"You can," Adam replied coyly, and Seán knew how he felt. The fish was still writhing; he didn't want to touch it either. He tugged on the line and, mercifully, the hook came out of its face without much resistance. Grabbing it around its middle, he threw its wet, cold body into the cooler as quickly as he could, and Adam slammed the lid on top of it. They could hear it bash itself against the inside of the box. Adam looked at it uncertainly.

"It's fine," Seán declared, wiping his hands on his jeans.

On the way home, they recounted the story of catching the fish. They laughed and told each other how they had felt and what it had looked like from their own perspectives, as if it had happened years ago. They were like old comrades, reminding each other of their adventures. By the time they pulled into the drive at home, the story had become more elaborate: the fish was three feet long, and together they had wrestled it fearlessly.

Seán lowered the tailgate and pulled the cooler toward them. He lifted the lid slowly, and they peered in at their spoils. It jumped. It jumped so ferociously that it cleared the walls of its cage and flew toward them. Seán leapt backwards with equal speed while pushing his son from the fish's trajectory so it narrowly avoided them, but all three ended up on the gravel.

For a moment, there was complete stillness. They stared at where the creature had landed, *surely* dead now, but it was the first of the group to move. Seán laughed unconvincingly and got to his feet. He reached his hand out to help Adam up but kept his eyes locked on the agitated fish. "Alright son?"

"I'm fine," Adam held his hand and stood, "it nearly got me."

"It's just a fish, couldn't have done any harm. Sorry, I overreacted there." He chuckled again.

"What do we do?"

We should kill it. We should kill it. We should kill it.

"We'll just leave it."

The fish had convulsed its way into the yard. The grass was a little overgrown, hiding it when it wasn't in the air.

"Leave it?"

"Leave it. Come on." Seán put his arm around Adam and steered him to the house. They both wanted to look back, but neither did. Once inside, Seán went into his bedroom and closed the door.

He lay down on his bed. He felt impotent. He got up again. He walked back into the living room and stood behind the sofa Adam was sitting in, watching television. He watched with him for a few minutes before the boy turned around.

"Alright?"

"Alright. Go take a look outside."

His son went obediently. Seán took his seat and changed the channel.

Adam was carrying the icebox when he came back in.

"It's in there?"

Adam shook his head. "It's still . . ."

Christ.

Adam put the icebox down and sat on the other sofa.

The sun was setting, but Seán didn't want to turn the lights on yet. One show ended, commercials came on. Mad adverts here, he thought. He'd never gotten used to them.

Adam looked over, "Shall I?"

Seán nodded. It must be time now.

The boy returned empty-handed.

More time passed, the sun had set. They were out of time. Seán stood up. "Get your coat."

Seán retrieved his shovel. Its wooden handle was worn, but the metal head looked new and sturdy. He joined Adam in the hall. He nodded at his son, his son nodded back, he opened the door. They walked into the darkness, past the truck and onto the grass. Adam led the way now; he knew where the fish was.

They arrived. It was finally dead. They waited a moment, to be sure.

Seán blessed himself. Like thieves, grateful for the darkness, they got to work. It was too late for anything else. They took turns digging.

When the hole was ready, Seán picked up the fish and placed it gently in its grave. They stared down at it for a moment.

"Do you want to say anything?"

Adam shook his head.

"Me neither, son."

Emissary on the Wall

Danae Younge

A painting hangs above our fireplace: in the high branches of a tranquil forest canopy, a girl spoons her back into the dipper of a hammock. Her eyes focus. For over a decade she's reread two pages in an unnamed book—as if our hometown wore brown wingtips & a blue blouse, reclined cozily in stillness. Memories are often found near ceilings.

It was after we moved south, the first time I noticed the ropes rocking slightly—appearing to sway with the teetering croak of mud toads, hammock stitching between sun curtains. Now I know her secret: not just that she breathes but that her book is an artifice. I could cleave it from her palms & find the leaves blank.

Now I notice how her ears perk up to eavesdrop, the spy, like poison weeping from the vial, like an antidote; every word we giggle into handfuls of midnight, hieroglyphic salt stains that whisper on the couch cushions, the shivers annexed from our minds during sleep.

One day I snipped flowers & freckled the living room floor—a funeral for all the unread pages. The next morning I found my boyfriend collecting the petals. He brewed them to make tea. While our tongues rolled sips of scorching chamomile like dice, I told him how I was free-falling in vacuous parchment, wind like aborted lyrics; an acrylic womb.

Cold Eggs

David Gambino

He woke to a boom.

Loudspeakers said it was a controlled detonation, some unexploded ordinance that needed to be disposed of. Most booms were uncontrolled. Taliban liked to wait until night to lob mortars at the airfield. IDF incoming, seek cover. Usually the shells landed harmlessly; people joked that it was like a blind outfielder trying to throw to home. Once in a while they killed someone. Whenever they hit before he woke up, he'd have to stay in his B-hut until someone came in and shined a flashlight on him. Accountability. Tonight, though, he didn't have to wait, so he groped his way through a dark maze of dust-cover blankets and plywood barriers with his toothbrush and towel.

The chow hall was more crowded than last deployment. There were four lines depending on what type of food you preferred at midnight: burgers and fries and other fast-food impersonations; leftover slop from dinner, probably chili-mac; a specialty line, the special always being grilled cheese; or breakfast, which was fake eggs and pancakes or French toast and generally the most palatable of the cuisines on offer. He queued for breakfast with others who shuffled along and held up their trays like Oliver Twists.

Are you flying? Tater asked with a mouthful of fake eggs. He was from Georgia and his last name sounded like tater-town. People imagined he called potatoes "taters," too, so the name stuck. Tater had been in the Navy and was now a defense contractor.

Yeah. You?

Just landed.

Anything exciting?

Same old.

He sat at twenty-thousand feet in the back of a Beechcraft King Air. It was a small twin prop airplane with a crew of four and loaded with equipment racks of computers and blinking lights. The neon glow inside the cabin combined with the hum of the engines was soothing. Mounted underneath the plane was a powerful video camera in the shape of a sphere that could rotate in any direction. He operated this ball with a hand controller.

The aircraft circled a small village in a ravine near the border with Pakistan for the next four hours. There were at least two military-aged males in the target compound, he knew, because another aircraft had followed them here a few days ago, watched them ride on a single moto like Jim Carrey and Jeff Daniels in *Dumb and Dumber*, just go, man. Shapes that weren't women or children were called mams on the radio. Since the mams came here, there was an aircraft above the compound at any given time, waiting for the moto to depart again. He didn't know who the targets were. He only knew them as black-hot blobs that sometimes woke up in the middle of the night to piss outside. The warm urine showed on his infrared camera until it wasn't warm anymore.

Status update?

Nothing to report, he answered.

Copy, the voice copied.

He had a unique relationship with the voice. He talked to it almost every night, which was more than he talked to his girlfriend or his parents or his coworkers. He had learned the subtle inflections the voice used and could tell when it was excited or angry or bored. It mostly sounded lonely, though. Someone had told him that the voices deploy for twelve months straight. They live in forward operating bases and communicate with intelligence collection aircraft via radio on behalf of the commanders. He felt a special bond with the voice because he was lonely, too.

The plane loitered long enough every night to witness an hour's worth of dawn. When it was bright enough, he pushed a button on his controller to switch from infrared to electro-optical, and the world below turned to color. He knew the two mams never left the compound in the morning. The most they ever did was walk across the courtyard and talk to one of three women living there. The women did all the chores. He watched them sweep the roof, hang laundry, get water from the village well. One of them seemed older and was probably a mother-in-law. He could tell by the way the mams' body language changed around her.

He counted four children. Their shapes were smaller than the adults' and they moved differently; they ran everywhere instead of walked. The adults never ran unless it was from a hellfire or guided bomb, in which case running was useless. He watched the children run from the compound to an open area south of a mosque where they joined eight others kicking a soccer ball. It looked fun, he thought.

Return eyes to target compound, the voice told him.

Copy, he copied.

Morning chow was open when he returned to base. The specialty line at breakfast was omelets made with real eggs, but the wait was much longer than the other lines. He told himself he'd wait for an omelet some other day. Today he ate the same food he'd eaten earlier, the same food he'd eaten every day for the last six months. He just shoveled it in. It didn't taste like anything anymore.

You flying today? the Colonel asked him with a mouthful of oatmeal. People called him the Colonel because he was an Air Force officer before becoming a contractor. Most of the others had been enlisted. They also told him it was because he looked like Colonel Sanders even though he didn't.

Just landed, he said. You?

Yeah. Going up soon. Anything exciting?

Same old.

He went to the Morale, Welfare, and Recreation center every day before bed. The building consisted of a makeshift theater with cushioned chairs and dim lighting. Half the uniformed audience would be asleep at any given time. The MWR also provided phones and wireless internet, slow as molasses. He watched *The Princess and the Frog* until he was tired enough to return to his B-hut.

The alarm on his watch woke him. He snuck with toothbrush and towel and walked fifty yards to the nearest latrine. He could smell it from twenty yards out. After he pissed, he climbed to the converted shipping container stacked on top. Warnings printed on computer paper and hung above the sinks told him not to exceed a four-minute shower, but he was alone and the water was hot today, so he allowed himself an extra two minutes.

Did you fly? he asked Tater at midnight chow through a mouth of French toast.

Just landed. You?

Same shift tonight. Anything exciting?

Same old.

He watched one of the mams take a shit at three in the morning. He zoomed in on the black-hot pile as close as the ball could go. He wanted to entertain the voice.

Describe the mam's activity, the voice played along.

Appears mam conducted biological and is returning to compound.

Copy. Let's zoom out one and return eyes to compound.

Wilco.

Dawn broke. The mams walked around the courtyard and occasionally one looked up and he wondered if they could see or hear his aircraft. The women swept the roof and boiled water over an outdoor fire. The children ran around.

Time to return to base.

He waited in the omelet line for ten minutes before deciding it wasn't worth it.

You fly this morning? asked the Colonel. A Polish sausage kept rolling away when he tried to stab it with a plastic fork.

Yeah, he said. You going up?

Yeah. Anything exciting?

Same old.

He went to the MWR and used the wifi to tell his girlfriend he missed her. He ate stale popcorn, a rare treat, and watched *Night at the Museum* until he was tired. He lay in bed and stared at the plywood ceiling and tried to recall all of the tiny decisions in his life that had brought him here.

Today is my down day, Tater said and bit into a bagel with cream cheese. Think I'll go to the MWR and call the wife and kids. You?

I'm flying, he said.

Have fun.

Put your eyes on the northeast corner of the courtyard, the voice said. Do you see a moto?

Can't break it out, he said. He tried adjusting the infrared contrast.

Copy. There should be a moto parked in that corner. We expect it to depart before dawn. Follow it when it departs.

Copy.

He kept his camera at max zoom and stared at the pixelated area for the next two hours. He started to question if there really was a moto. Maybe it had left before he came on station and they had missed it. He blinked the fatigue from his eyes when two black shapes appeared in the courtyard.

Have activity in corner of courtyard, he said. Two mams.

Copy, said the voice. We have a pred on station. Intent is kinetic strike when moto departs the village.

Copy.

He could hear his pulse quicken inside his headset. His bladder tightened. The pilots said Finally, some fucking action.

Moto departing southbound, he said. Two mams onboard.

Copy. Call out collateral damage concerns every ten seconds.

His palm was sweaty against the hand controller. He zoomed out, careful to maintain the black dot at the top of his screen. It picked up speed once it cleared the village. He looked ahead for any structures or other black shapes.

Collateral damage no factor, he said. He counted to ten.

Collateral damage no factor. He counted to ten.

Collateral damage no factor.

Rifle, a new voice said.

He followed the moto for several more seconds until it disappeared in a flash of black, the ensuing dust cloud appearing in the span of a single frame and obscuring the ball's field of view. He zoomed in and waited for the dust and smoke to dissipate.

Haji ain't walking away from that one, a pilot said.

Maintain this field of view and report any movement, the voice told him.

Copy.

When the area cleared, all he could see was a small scattering of black shapes. He couldn't make out anything that looked like a moto or a person.

No movement, he said.

He waited in line and asked for cheese, tomatoes, jalapeños, and onions in his omelet. He sat down and watched the news on one of the chow hall televisions. The President announces new troop surge, it said. After a while, the Colonel came and sat across from him.

Anything exciting? The Colonel asked.

He looked down at his cold, uneaten eggs.

Same old.

Breaking These Lines Apart

Amie Heisserman

I'm not a fisherman. But I stand here, pulling nets from the water, taking my knife and cutting the line, dismantling each ropey ring, unweaving the woven web, watching fish drop back into the water: silver plops, a swish and ripple, then gone. I trace where the ropes have burned my hand, trying to follow the lines they've made, to see how they cross the lines already there. I'll cast these fragments back on shore, and watch where they fall, knowing I don't know what these broken lines mean.

Creative Nonfiction Second Prize

A Fragile Inheritance

Lora Straub

Grammar sits at the head of her dining room table, two inches of chianti in her favorite "glass," a small plastic juice cup. She uses this slim, clear five-ounce cup for water, wine, and Coca Cola, which she prefers flat and room temperature. Dinner is done, and the humid August air is loosened by electric fans. We're eating Grammar's favorite dessert—Swedish cream, a solid pudding made with sour cream, heavy cream, vanilla, sugar and gelatin-boiled and set in small Pyrex dishes, topped with sugared raspberries. Aunt Margaret made it, and it's cool and rich, like the air conditioning Grammar doesn't have. Gale and I sit adjacent, Mom and Aunt Margaret sit across, Uncle Jim sits opposite Grammar, reigning patriarch and matriarch of the family, respectively.

Gale and I are 18. We leave for college soon. We're Grammar's youngest grandchildren. Mom is 50, Uncle Jim and his wife Margaret are 57. Grammar is 82. These are the good times, gathered around her dining room table. Gale and I sit, our bare feet brushing the thick gold carpet. We listen, smile, repeat. We could be bored as this evening winds down, but we're not. Our cheeks hurt from smiling. Uncle Jim talks about his time at Brown University, where I'm headed to join the cross-country team; Aunt Margaret tells stories about our cousins Catherine and Joe, their two adult children; and Mom tries to get a word in edgewise. Grammar talks about death.

She's talking, again, about her Waterford crystal that fills the wall-length china cabinet behind my back. It's the only room in the house besides the kitchen that isn't lined with bookshelves—there are only two, stuffed with cookbooks, along the shorter edges of the rectangular room. Her record player is to the right of her, with a rubber model of the California Raisins rocking out atop it. When she leaves the house, she blasts opera to deter robbers.

"When I die," Grammar says to me, "You and Gale will each get half of the Waterford. Margaret has already claimed the crystal lamp with its chandelier shade." This lamp watches us on the buffet table in front of a mirror, next to yet another bowl of fake fruit lightly shrouded in dust. I catch Gale's eyes in the mirror, roll my own and sigh.

"Why do you always talk about when you're gone?" I ask. "I don't want to talk about that."

I'm ignored. I continue, "I'd rather get nothing and not talk about it."

"You say that now," Grammar says primly. "Not everyone feels that way." The candles flicker. I feel bad for feeling bad. The Waterford radiates behind my back. It is lit from inside the cabinet. When Grammar is dead, half of it is mine. Blood crystal. Dread crystal. But not for years and years, I think. Mom puts on the water for tea. Grammar wails, "Am I Having A Good Time?"

"You're having a good time, Mother," Uncle Jim responds drolly.

We all laugh. This is one of her jokes, making fun of her age and mind, and best--one in which her son partakes.

My outburst is forgotten. I sit, smile, glow, fester. When Uncle Jim and Aunt Margaret leave for their apartment, and Mom, Gale, and I go to bed, I can't sleep. I'm in the twin bed I always sleep in. I can smell the books in the giant bookcase parallel. If I reach out, I could brush the spines with my fingertips. I hear Grammar downstairs washing the dishes. Even though she has a dishwasher, she handwashes each one, then dries it, puts it away. She rinses Romaine lettuce the same way—each leaf bathed individually, diligently patted dry with a piece of paper towel like she has all the time in the world. No salad is lint-free. Dinner is served notoriously late, with everyone starving but Grammar, who never seems hungry. When she's done, she watches disasters unfold on CNN, unable to sleep. Dishes and disasters slip in and out of my consciousness.

This is a scene I remember well, stronger for its recurrence, like numerous coats of nail polish, unchipped. Eight years later, Grammar died, and Mom and Aunt Katie did the tedious work of splitting up and packing Grammar's Waterford crystal. Gale and I were 26 and, though we had several upper-education degrees between us, we weren't trusted with packing up this fragile inheritance that I (and Gale, to a lesser extent) had long eschewed. I didn't *want* that responsibility, per se, I just wanted to be trusted, seen as trustworthy, but I wasn't—callously, I'd threatened to sell it.

"The Waterford really was precious to her," Mom said. "There were even a few broken pieces in the cabinet, pushed to the back. She couldn't bear to throw them away."

"Mom. She couldn't bear to throw *anything* away."

Mom stored the crystal at her home in the guest room closet for the warmer months, and moved it into Dad's light-filled closet for the drafty winters. She kept it safe until Gale and I were each stable enough in our lives—i.e., we both ended up in colonial New England houses with built-in china cabinets. Now we each have sparkling half-sets of Waterford completely at odds with the rest of our belongings that will make moving anywhere unduly stressful. When my husband and I unboxed them, six years after Grammar's death, Steve unwrapped each with reverence. Held one after the other up to the light and admired the cut. I buried my nose in a goblet like I was smelling a flower, still caught a whiff of mildewed books and Grammar's warm presence in the stale air caught between the glass and newspaper. Perhaps the stemware summoned the scent.

It had nothing to do with trust. Wrapping that crystal was one of the last things Mom could do for her mother, and that doubled as a gift for her daughters: the unwrapping. Grammar's house, most of her books, dishtowels, the gold carpet, her fake fruit: all gone. But the scent: a momentary return of a singular spirit.

Grammar was right, of course—I am glad to have the glasses: old-fashioned cups, goblets, tumblers. Glasses for sherry, for white wine, and water. One vase, one bowl. I didn't know how glad, until I broke one right away, a whiskey tumbler with a thick cut bottom and thin etched rim. While washing it, my hands jerked up, seemingly on their own, not unlike a Ouija board's gliding planchette, touched, the glass smashed into the faucet. The pieces stayed on the windowsill behind the sink for weeks, the delicate shards of crystal piled atop each other like wet rose petals, shining, until I pushed them into a paper bag. I don't want to keep what's broken, even if it's beautiful. Though she was deathly serious about her Waterford, it's not what made her valuable, not even close.

When Steve and I use the Waterford, we clink the crystal softly, and I see Grammar's infectious smile, hear her musical laugh. I joke about death, too. It's not time to be serious, yet.

Mom kept Grammar's true favorite glass, bequeathed to no one--the small plastic juice cup, holder of water, chianti, and flat, room-temperature Coca Cola.

The House

Atreyee Gupta

In the morning
cabinet doors are petulant—
squeaking in protest at the
interruption—
drawers too—
belligerent about disruption.
I leave them ajar
to breathe.
The house waits—
to be washed
to be fed
to be—
cajoled into being.

Hours stretch—
light creeping between slitted blinds
barring across floorboards
grazing stucco—
to passing years.
I sweep
I dust—
still—
specks float
settle—
ocean threatening to bury me.

Outside the window
the crow urges—
stay wild, stay wild!
I hover over stove—
face aflame
half-a-mind on the branch.
Words lurk in paneled wood—
expecting to be poems.

Days tumble—
devoured by distractions.
Halls become tunnels
through which my life
walks without me.

Shadows gather under sills—
sulking for inspiration.
So many rooms
to nurse—
not a single one mine.

Finally
darkness settles—
I watch the purple mood grow.
Drapes quiver
from a ghost breeze.
House stretches—
yawns—
before sinking in repose.
I hear the faint pulsate of its heart—
ta-thump, ta-thump, ta-thump—
echo of my wings
beating upon the unlit lamp.

At last—
secrets chased
back into their compartments—
necessities
stored for another day—
I stare at the canvas
searching for some chore
to take away the pain
of an empty brain.

Gravity Pajamas

Claire Bateman

After so much suffering, all those failed attempts at a cure, the only treatment for the global insomnia crisis turned out to be direct skin contact with jewels and precious stones.

Now, thanks to the collaboration of geologists and fashion engineers, everyone can recover in sleepwear woven from micro-processed sapphires, emeralds, rubies, garnets, pearls, those little luminosities extracted from the earth and her waters.

Because the shaped, made-to-measure garment itself is far too heavy to lift, as though its fibers strain to return to the lithosphere, it's wheeled into your bedroom on a dolly, then deposited by a crane-like device onto your massively fortified bed. At the end of the day, you maneuver yourself awkwardly into its opening; when the alarm rings, or in the night hours when you need to respond to the demands of passion, your bladder, or a restless baby, you work your way out of that mineral carapace, leave it glittering on the sheets.

Though this is inconvenient, it's certainly preferable to the trauma of collective wakefulness, which was so terrible that people don't speak of it except on rare occasions, and even then, only by euphemism and indirection. Nor do they talk about their sleep, commenting on its quality or recounting dreams; a new diffidence prevails, like the shyness of lovers reunited after an epic absence, as the one who stayed behind, noticing subtle changes in the other, wonders if this is indeed the longed-for union, or perhaps something else entirely.

In Front of the Full-Length Mirror

Jennifer Lang

1. Divot, Lower Leg, 2016

The summer of my fifty-second birthday, I detect a blotch with dark uneven borders, freeze the image on my cellphone camera, and e-mail it to my dermatologist.

Within hours, Dr. Shapiro responds: *call office for referral to get removed immediately.* When I remind him of my upcoming quarterly scan, he writes: *No. Get removed. Now.*

Two stitches and fourteen days of daily bandage changes later, on a sauna-hot summer day in the center of Israel, my phone rings: *"Jennifer, ze melanoma."*

The M word snaps me to attention. Dr. Shapiro explains what to do—*letapel, lahzor, lehorid:* to treat, to return, to remove. My brain stops simultaneous translation. I switch to English and put him on speaker phone so my husband Philippe can hear. Too many heavy, frightening, foreign words.

My greatest fear: my sensitive, fair, freckled skin maligning no matter how much I protect it.

Dermatological incisions and I go way back. My first occurred in a very sexy spot: mid-buttocks circa 1995. Since then, thanks to familial history and a light complexion inherited from a long line of Eastern European Jewish ancestors, several other extractions have followed: right knee; right toe; left forearm; right forehead; left eye. All benign.

Until this. Skin cancer. Nine new stitches. A five-millimeter margin. Mean and deep like a dog bite.

I take responsibility for some of my scars, consequences of youth and ignorance. Everyone in my northern California hometown sunbathed. In the late '70s, my pre-teen friends and I lay on chaise lounges in our backyard, our fronts and backs doused in Johnson's Baby Oil. They tanned. I scorched. My skin raged a wildfire red that hurt to touch before white, water-filled blisters formed then peeled.

Decades later, I visit the dermatologist every three months. Each time, he inspects my body against 125 naked photos of me taken in New York. When I had told my American dermatologist about our upcoming move to Israel, she'd said, "Just remember to stay out of the sun." I half-laughed, half-cried. Didn't she know Israel is a desert?

Following last summer's biopsy results, I undergo cancer staging evaluation: specialized eye exam and in-depth lymph node ultrasounds in my breasts, neck, and groin. On every referral, Hebrew words, myriad numbers, and eight letters in English: melanoma. When results return clean and clear, Dr. Shapiro explains I have melanoma in situ—on the top layers of the skin or stage 0 or pre-cancer. A longtime yoga practitioner, I exhale deeply for the first time in weeks.

2. Pinkish-greyish Streak, Lower Abdomen, 2003

My belly flops over a four-inch line, a division between my upper and lower body, between life and death. To see it, I press in, lift up, peer down. Every April fifteenth, I silently commemorate the event—unbearable pelvic pain, several fainting spells, emergency CT scan, multiple and frantic gynecologist and gastroenterologist appointments—culminating in my doctor's urgent call: "We missed it earlier. Meet me in the ER, *a.s.a.p.!*"

My intrauterine device—a copper wire, hormone-free form of contraception—had gone awry: a less-than-one percent chance. A fertilized egg implanted *outside* my uterus in a fallopian tube. As soon as I awakened after a life-saving blood transfusion and laparotomy to remove a ruptured tube, I glimpsed our pediatrician and next-door neighbor making rounds.

"You're lucky to be here," Dr. David said. "You could have died."

Apparently, I'd been bleeding internally for two weeks when the ache first struck. My neighbor's words stunned me—into silence, submission, surrender. No matter how well I ate, how much I exercised, or how often I practiced yogic breath, my inner workings were beyond my control.

After the initial shock faded, after I walked to the bathroom unaccompanied, after I returned home for a six-week recovery, I became enraged. I blamed the company that fabricated the faulty IUD, the doctors who misdiagnosed me, my body for betraying me. Called a lawyer to determine if I had a case. Wrote a letter to my ob-gyn detailing my pain and suffering. Told the story ad nauseam to everyone within earshot.

Yet, anger aside, I had perspective. As excruciating as my near-death experience had been, it wasn't life-long or life-threatening. It wasn't like that of an old high school classmate, Annie, who also suffered from dire pelvic pain. Every time I'd complained to my mother about my symptoms, she'd update me about Annie. Diagnosed with ovarian cancer at age thirty-seven, Annie died eighteen months later, leaving behind two children the same ages as mine.

When my gynecologist examined me at my first post-op appointment, she admired her handiwork. "The incision's beautiful," she boasted. It would be several more years, several more interventions for me to see it her way. Still, I whispered words of thanks—to her and to it, my savior in disguise.

Before surgery, I'd felt invincible. So much stronger than my younger self. A newly certified yoga instructor, I could carry any load on my developing biceps, could hike the hills with my long hamstrings. Ancient breath techniques calmed my overzealous mind.

After surgery, I couldn't hoist myself out of my hospital bed and cried, convinced the doctors had removed all four of my abdominal muscles. During my recovery, I understood the truth behind my yoga teacher's words; our bodies are merely a skeleton, an outer shell. That shell is separate from everything inside. Then, and only then, did I realize the real meaning: I will die, but my soul will live on.

3. Six White Marks, Wrist, 2012

One Saturday morning in southwestern France, I followed Philippe alongside the tide pools, slipped on algae, heard a sharp snap, and rode in a wailing ambulance to the local clinic. After surgery to repair my bent, broken radius bone, the on-call doctor discharged me, saying "*Il faut que vous soyez Zen.*" Two weeks later, back in Israel and still in agony and far from Zen, an orthopedist recommended another operation to remove the poorly placed pins, reinsert new ones, and reset the bones.

At Laniado Hospital, I shook. Intense, uncontainable spasms. Philippe stroked me like a cat. I ranted about the Old World waiting room and cheap plastic chairs and stomach-turning stench of over-boiled potatoes. He shushed me like a newborn baby. I closed my eyes and summoned three-part yoga breath, inhaling belly, ribs, chest. But sometimes the mystical practice, whether the pranayama or the philosophical mumbo jumbo, rang false. Irrational fear overpowered everything else.

At home, a friend offered help. Dirty and desperate to shower, I couldn't do anything alone. She carefully slid my nightshirt over my head, while I single-handedly yanked off my underwear. She turned on the water. I checked the temperature. She held the soap and shampoo. I stepped into the stall, holding my arm outside the door to keep the cast dry.

Despite my state of undress and my cumulation of cicatrices, I've always been comfortable with my form and frame. Perhaps because I was born and raised in the everything-goes Bay Area or because my parents used to prance around in the raw at home or because my mother lectured on the importance of changing clothes openly in the middle school locker room. "We're all women and at some point our bodies will look alike," she reminded me before every new school year.

But, no matter how much I accepted my body's blemishes, I battled with my mind and its hell-bent need for control. I warred with the what-ifs. What if the second surgeon couldn't correct the first surgeon's error? What if I couldn't write or practice yoga professionally without pain? What if next time something worse happened?

Banned from grocery shopping, cooking, texting, typing, and driving, I did little more than watch movies, read books, or listen to music. In that unfamiliar, unstructured, Zen-like territory, I pondered how motherhood, yoga, and time had reshaped muscle, fat, and bone. How my scars had formed a new legend, reformed my body's topography. How borders had shifted where skin was marred, soft, supple, sagging, taut, tender, toned. How other, less tangible borders between here, now and there, then had started to blur.

4. Inch-long Line, Breast, 1995

I was thirty, married, and the mother of a toddler when the gynecologist palpated my left breast twice as long as my right during a routine examination. She told me they were dense and fatty, fibroid cystic, words with which I was familiar thanks to my mother, who had had a lump removed when I was in fifth grade. The doctor's fingers circled repeatedly in both directions. She stopped and said, "You have a small cyst," leaving no time to respond. She explained the plan of action: ultrasound, mammogram, fine-needle aspiration. Every result pointed toward biopsy. Philippe accompanied me to the clinic, squeezing my hand while I beseeched my heart to stop hammering, my stomach to stop somersaulting. New to yoga, I had not yet cultivated breath control techniques. I lacked self-soothing mechanisms. I had no words for impermanence, mortality.

When the skin healed normally, despite a dozen very fine stitches, I was relieved. When the doctor's report revealed that the growth was benign, I exhaled, deep, long, all-encompassing.

An image of Merrill, my mother's best friend, floated into my mind. Merrill with her coarse, dyed hair, her gravelly voice, a cigarette always dangling from her mouth, in her hands an espresso. Merrill, who had been like my second mother. Merrill, diagnosed with breast cancer in her early fifties. Merrill, who suffered complications and countless surgeries and four years later died.

Death is like looking in the mirror, seeing our deeper selves, the bare-bones truths. I am dying: my wounds evidence of this promise. They remind me of my fragility, my inability to stop nature.

5. Adjoining Scars, Shoulder, Early '80s

Keloid, Dr. Dotz had called it: excess scar tissue where the skin has healed after an injury, less common among Caucasians like myself. I'd always been the exception when it came to skin.

I confessed to Dr. Dotz that I'd probably picked pimples or irritated mosquito bites, maybe in high school or college, and begged surgical removal. "Only if you want them to grow back bigger," he'd said. I have no choice but to live with the jagged, Bazooka pink, elevated scars, which, together, form the shape of a mini footprint.

Sometimes I run my left fingers over them. Sometimes Dr. Shapiro rubs them during my quarterly scans, examining the keloids as well as the freckles scattered in and under and around them with a specialized lens, and asks if they bother me. I tell him they itch on occasion. They appear harmless.

"It's part of your charm," Philippe once said about my spotty complexion. He reassures me the keloids came with the package. The package, I remind him, has changed. Broken down. Fallen apart. Undergone repair. Looks different. Feels different. The antonym of in situ: disturbed.

Occasionally before bed, I pause in front of the full-length mirror in my room, looking at my body's map, comparing Philippe's view of the goods against mine. Do my markings make me feel less feminine or more flawed? Before, when I was younger, yes. Now, what I once saw as defects, I see as badges, souvenirs of my experiences and proof of my resilience. I could never pose for *Elle* or *Shape* magazine, but I can speak to people about imperfection and fear and self-acceptance.

My body tells stories about a girl who grows up to be a woman who grows up to become a wife who grows up to become a mother who grows up to understand her humanity. My body tells stories, and I am determined to listen to every one of them for as long as I can.

Fogless

Gianna Sannipoli

The morning turned silver.
The highway, blue as I drove through it,
was busy with cars too fast—
women and men
on their way to God.
Shell game,
ugly wrap
tactic for life.
I want a room—
clean pink,
conflated bouquets
neither stolen nor bought.
Grown in any month but March.
An identity
less hyacinth
and more baby's breath,
white as the
dripping vanity,
faceless mirror.
Less life,
more God.
And the sun
so persistent,
that I wake to it
and am forced to say
I am excited about God
so I am excited about life.
But a fogless Sunday morning
is all we can really ask for
and probably all we'll ever get.
When you pretended to love me,
I was more lust than loss,
and now, more doubt than faith.

I want to wake up
as anything.
A mouse, a bridge,
a believer, a Florence-perfected
antique sad iron
with a stay-cool handle.
Anything
other than
a godless girl
you no longer love.

Heartwood

Sarah McCartt-Jackson

She forgot what it felt like to climb the oak tree out front, to dissect the decaying, half-eaten acorns by splitting the shell with her fingernail, feeling what was left of the meat thatch her heart like the inside of an acorn cap. She tried to remember how to throw her ankle over the branch then pull herself up into the crook, her bare legs in jean shorts scratching against the bark. And how it felt to test each limb before putting her weight on it, how to hold the middle trunk like a mainmast in the crow's nest. She thought if she could remember that one small space where a branch had broken off, where it left a hole that healed over itself, she might be able to remember the things she put inside: four clover blossoms tied together at the stem, a gray bird feather the size of her pinky bone, one dead ant. She felt for the way a summer thunderstorm would come, wind first, then electric-colored clouds. She thought about what her father's face looked like when he looked up and saw her there in the tree, limb-swung and alive. He couldn't remember her face, only her small body lying on the grass, dress ruffle fluttering, leg bent.

The Line

Jonathan McLelland

The trick was not lifting the pencil. Jim gripped the yellow Number 2 pencil tightly in his left hand and pressed his left cheek to the white paper tablecloth. He took a breath and held it. He squeezed his right eye shut, and began pushing the pencil forward, not touching the table with his arm, sighting along the grey line with his left eye as the tip of the pencil stuttered toward the salt shaker.

From his spoon's-eye vantage, the clear glass salt shaker with the bright chrome head stood like a tower. As the pencil tip drew near, Jim held it still for a long moment, glancing away to his right from the drawn line, four inches clockwise to another tower, the pepper shaker.

It would have been too easy to touch at one corner of the salt shaker, or even to trace two sides off the hexagon, and then push off toward the black tower. If he'd had to say why he didn't want to encircle the salt shaker, he'd have said *Because,* meaning that it would have been inelegant. He'd thought of it, of course, but the idea gave him a hollow feeling in the pit of his stomach, and he dismissed it instantly.

Tracing the near half of the salt shaker's hexagonal base was clearly the right move, and he did that. It was surprisingly delicate work. He got as close to the edge of the glass shaker as he could without touching the pencil to it. Going slowly was an obvious tactic, and he used it, but he wanted his line to be as straight as possible, and pushing a pencil tip-first across paper—especially without resting your arm on the table—is tricky business. The paper covering the table top wasn't smooth. It was slightly bumpy, embossed with a mottled texture, like ancient papery leather from an animal that died with a rash. The pencil point naturally wanted to grab at the surface, or to burrow its point into the paper. Besides that, from Jim's one-eyed tabletop view, there was a visual threshold only a few inches out, past which the world flattened and loomed, and distances became very hard to judge.

Jim pushed his pencil tip out across the wide expanse of white paper toward the pepper shaker. Only an inch out, he felt a moment of something like panic, as a vertiginous loss of depth perception gripped him, and he thought for a moment that his pencil might suddenly jab headlong into the pepper shaker. He stopped his hand and let out a long, slow breath. His mother and her friend paused in mid-sentence to look down at him. Jim was unaware of the women's appraising stare, and did not notice the second-long pause in the conversation passing across the table above his head. He drew in another breath and held it.

Each measure of distance closed was more difficult than the previous. That meant going slower and slower the closer he got to the pepper. But then, as suddenly as it had come upon him, the past moment's anxiety left him completely, and Jim's face flushed warm with the wonderful rightness of the pencil's journey. With the quiet exhilaration of absolute confidence, he rode the grey line toward the pepper shaker, which seemed to grow as he approached it, and to loom clifflike from the paper. As he drove nearer to the glass face than another might have dared—just when an onlooker, certain of a crash, would have drawn a sharp breath, Jim, using only the muscles of his left shoulder, altered the pencil's tack, conning it smoothly past the vertex of the pepper shaker's farthest corner and into open space, out toward the edge of the table.

If the table had been larger, and if no one else had been there to bother him, if there had been no shakers or cutlery or sugar bowl on the table, if he had been all alone, that's when Jim would have pushed his pencil right out into the white space, arcing it and looping it, tracing the paper with nothing but unconcerned flow. He could have lost himself in it, riding the line as the pencil and the paper welcomed it, and there'd have been no chance of catching the tip or tearing the paper, because he could have felt the connection between the pencil and the paper and followed it.

Jim felt all of that for the first two inches after he left the pepper shaker behind. And it only took that moment's indulgence, pushing the pencil forward with his mind's eye on the imaginary wide open paper, for the table to remind him just how tenuous his position was. The bright glow of the imagined paper snapped off like an electric light as the pencil tip passed suddenly out of Jim's sight, his view blocked by the bridge of his own nose. And the disappearance came with the equally sudden knowledge that the now-invisible pencil point might be a hair's breadth from the edge of the table, the line careering blindly toward oblivion.

He stopped. As if waking suddenly from a deep sleep in the middle of a dream, Jim sucked in his breath. His left shoulder blazed, and he felt cold and nauseatingly disoriented. But, of course! Stopping had made it all right. His shoulder hurt, but he could stand that. As long as he didn't move the tip of the pencil to his right, everything was fine. Jim pulled a long, slow breath.

His mother stopped again. Jim heard her say something to her friend, but he only registered it as a close-by rising and falling tone, a familiar color against the blurred and clattering auditory landscape.

Obviously, he could not *pull* the pencil. That would be wrong. With his left arm wrapped nearly around his head, barely able to push his hand forward, and with the still-unseen tip held tightly against the paper, Jim slowly rotated the pencil with his fingertips, levering it gently to the right. Then, with a cramped backhand motion, he began carefully to push the line to the left. When the graphite tip reappeared from behind the cloudbank of his nose, Jim's cheeks flushed again, warmer and pinker this time. He closed his left eye and let the breath out through his nose while his heartbeat slowed.

When he opened his eye again, he drew another deliberate breath and surveyed the terrain back to his left. In the middle distance, a single drop of water was slowly flattening as the stiff paper unwillingly absorbed it. Jim felt a slight misgiving even as he confirmed to himself that there was no reasonable alternative to heading for the drop, but the certain need for decisiveness overrode the qualm, and he pushed the scratching tip forward.

The first couple of inches required no more than his now-practiced vigilance, and he managed to steer the tip with no risk of tearing the paper. Within half an inch of the drop, however, the situation altered dramatically. Somewhere between there and the shore of the flattening dome, the paper would be soaked. If the tip crossed that boundary, it would instantly burrow through the sodden pulp and straight into the wood of the table. But there could be no question of irresolution. Jim pushed the tip steadily toward the point that he judged to be the closest safe approach, and then he tacked smoothly to the right, circling east of the drop and its soggy shoals, pushing counterclockwise halfway around the drop before pushing out onto clear, dry paper to the north.

Jim longed to push off to the left, to explore the unknown paper to the northwest, where he knew a glistening water glass towered above the surface with a great spreading ring of damp around it. But it was impossible. He couldn't see clearly enough that far to the left without moving his head, and that was out of the question. It was clear to him that only one path lay open: he had no choice but to head due north toward the sugar bowl, to navigate around its southeastern edge, and then push back toward the familiar shape of the salt shaker. He felt slightly wistful at the thought, but also satisfied, as he imagined ending his journey almost where he'd started, stopping the tip, laying the pencil down, and surveying the unbroken grey line of his voyage.

But then, with a bright, cold horror that squeezed his stomach, he remembered the near-fatal consequence of his last bout of daydreaming, the sense of panic that had almost overcome him when the tip had disappeared behind his nose. This time, though, there was no sharp intake of breath. Experience had inured him to overreaction, and his mother and her friend talked on, oblivious to his moment of inner turmoil. Without missing a beat, Jim pushed steadily toward the worn white ceramic of the sugar bowl. Sachets of white, yellow, pink, and blue paper edged neatly above the rectangular bowl's rim as Jim pushed the yellow Number 2 pencil north.

There was an embossed ridge a couple of inches from the bowl—nothing insurmountable, but a hazard to be negotiated nevertheless—and Jim risked a glance to his right, checking the position of the distant salt shaker as he broached the ridge, so that he'd be ready for it on the final approach to the shaker's base. Two more inches or so would be close enough to the bowl's steeply sloping sides—not too close, or he'd never manage the course change without pulling—and he could begin his angled arc to the northeast, just a broad reflection of the sugar bowl's corner, enough to make clear that he'd done as he intended before heading home, and then *"Here we go! Pancakes!"* and his mother tugged the pencil from his hand.

The sound struck him. There was no time to gasp or to cry out, no time even to raise his arms. His mother's hand was on his shoulder, pushing him back in his seat, as the waitress cleared the salt and pepper away with her right hand and set the plate of pancakes on the paper in front of him with her left. So many tables to take care of, she was gone before the cutlery's brief ring had finished, while the thump of the heavy white plate still filled Jim's head. She never saw his face. Wholly without malice or comprehension, Jim's mother forgot the look on his face almost the instant she saw it. Her friend did see it, and recognized in it much more than she knew how to name, settling for *He is such a strange child.*

In that hot frozen moment, the shock of the plate's thump flooded Jim's body with a certain knowledge: before now he'd have cried, but today he would not. And because he would not, nothing would ever be the same again.

Lady of Bone Writing

Kym Cunningham

shewas whatcutsdeeper thanether thatwhichhas alreadybeendealt sheemerged inalphabets asletters cametoher exchangingonefor anotherliketheywould oiled metal oneforbread twoforwine herpensaltandsmokeher inksheetched syllables withcalligraphy ofthefinestblade shesuffered nomiddlinglanguage favoringthe mandible forits mobiusstrip sothattheturn erasedthedust ofantecedents inhisto ry writtenoveritself shewasthesite atwhich pastandfuture didnotmerge somuch ascease toholdmeaning sheshowedthe mythofprogress forwhatitwas someatte mpt todelineatewhat camebefore fromthatwhich wascoming rightatthem acase ofmistakenidentity likehowthey lookedatafibula andsaw astraightline asticktop ick theearthsteeth butsheknew itwasntline orevenbone itwasinfinite anunendin gsurface andthepressure requiredforemphasis layinthe matterofstrength orresili ence orrefusaltoletup amatterof willingnesstocompress somethingsofragile lon gago shehadlearned thevanityofweight thedestructionwroughtbyexcess thatsh owbonescrumble andallislost butshemourned notbecause itwasalwaysalready lost sheofferednotjustice butsomethingclose toapathy inthatwhatwastaken was notpath butlabyrinthaskeletal engravingwithneither beginningnor endwhateve ntually wouldcease tobelike herself shewasold butcouldntremember howshego tthatway beingborn cracked andbroken ifshewasever reallybornatall shetook n otime forwonder she hadsomuch towrite somanybones togetherstories wouldn everbedeciphered shewasnt oraclebutprophesy shadowingbackandfore shewas anarchive oferosion ananagram toberepositioned forendless newmeaning liket hespell ofhowbone comesfrombeing andthebane ofwhat thissignified thetauto logicalanswer whennostatement isthesame impossible andforthat shecouldntb eallowed theywere unsureafterall ifshewasghost orsomethingelseentirely theyc ouldntguessthat shewasneither theinbetween liminalofallthings hunchbacked withscapulaepushed sofarout tolookwinged theycouldnotabide hercurvature t heycame forher intheday resolving tobreak herstraight theyput her onthewheel pulledher betweentwohorses asthoughshewererope butshejustcoiled tighterout ofplace frustratedthem whenherpieces wouldntfitbacktogether and

them ore herb od y frac tur ed them ore shepl intered in tosy nech do che but j agg eda nd mean in glesss he turne di nan do verb e coming t hes pi rale nd less lyre ar range d asp a li mp sest o fbro ken sel fan dint his un ten able bodys hew on dere d wh at curs ewe car vea n din w hat ma terial

Dying Back

Patrick Cabello Hansel

I run the red and green push
mower over the back yard one
more time; less to cut what little
grass remains than to chop the weed
tree leaves browning up on the
Creeping Charlie and crabgrass.
Tonight, we will cover the tomatoes
and peppers in a quixotic hope of
squeezing a few more gifts from
October. Small green tomatoes hang
from withering vines. The raspberry
canes bend down, laden with almost-fruit.

In the front yard, our silver maple
and gingko hold onto their green
like visas against death, while
the fiery maples across the street
jettison their crimson fingers into
this fierce wind. It will be useless
to rake for days. Our leaves will
fly to the neighbor's, the neighbor's
to ours. Already the hostas and
sunflowers are shedding their bones,
and the flowers the bees delighted
in all summer have shrunken to seed.

All this is ordered by an ancient
call: earth and her creatures
loosing what they love to die back
into winter. Every fall, they take
the cup and drink it. Every autumn
their goodbyes ravish our eyes

with color. Maybe a tree weeps
each leaf she has held as it drops
down to rot away. I cannot know.
But there is welcome for each in
the deep dark where roots labor
among the blind beasts. It may be
that each fallen leaf, each withered
stalk dancing and dying is a tender
of incense, a prayer flag, a knee
bent to offer blessing to the world.

Not Naming It

Shuly Xóchitl Cawood

The cat came with the farm. A stipulation.

"I don't want a cat," Marisol told her husband, Elton, who was the one working with the realtor, who in turn represented the woman—elderly, widowed—selling the farm.

"It's fine," he told the realtor. "We'll take the cat."

"I'm not petting it," Marisol said. "Or feeding it."

"I'll feed it," he said.

"It lived in the house. I don't want it in the house."

"There's always the barn," Elton said.

The cat was black, and this concerned Marisol. *No lo toques*, her mother would have said. Black cats were bad luck, curses. They portended beautiful things that could be marred by misfortune.

"This is a fresh start for us," Elton said. It's why he had quit his job and why he'd pushed for the farm in the first place. They had always been city dwellers, living in a tiny apartment on the ninth floor of a high-rise, accustomed to a market on every corner, subways and museums and takeout close by, commuting a handful of blocks to their jobs. Trading all that in for a property with none of the conveniences and all of the work? Everyone thought they were crazy. Marisol thought they were crazy. But Elton promised she would be happy. She wanted to believe him, but she didn't.

"We'll grow our own food," Elton said. But Marisol was tired of growing things.

"We'll love the quiet," he said, but noise was all she wanted. Her mind was now too fallow.

They packed up their apartment and moved out one February morning. It took them seven hours to get to the farm, and by the time they did, darkness had invaded the property. Marisol looked at it and thought, *more of the same.*

"I'm done for the day," she said before they even got out of the moving truck. "I'm going to bed."

He fished the key to their new life from his pocket. "Sure," he said. "We can get our stuff out tomorrow."

Elton was easier on her now, not pushing her the way he used to—not spurring her on to work harder, get up earlier, go with him to the gym, lobby for that promotion. She had taken a cut in her salary to move here, since she would be working remotely, unable to meet clients in person, only able to do the backend work, the drone-like tasks she used to hate but were all she could tolerate these days. People couldn't see the stain on her heart. They thought she wasn't different. She was. She didn't want to see people anymore. She didn't want to hear about their vacations and their children and soccer games and recitals and graduations, and she especially didn't want to hear about how their kids were driving them bananas.

At least they had bananas.

The cat was not in the house. The cat was nowhere to be seen for the first four days as they unloaded and unpacked and wiped down shelves and washed walls and swept floors and pushed their belongings into the old widow's closets.

"Maybe it's gone for good," Marisol said. "Fine with me."

"It'll be back." Elton stirred the bucket of paint so he could start on the walls of their new house, which wasn't new at all. It was older than they were, having witnessed a century of stories: beginnings, middles, ends.

Elton said, "It's probably hiding in the barn."

He was right. The cat appeared one Sunday morning outside the barn door. Marisol saw it from the kitchen window after she snatched the skillet from the brown stove and scraped eggs into the sink—eggs she had burned, like everything else. "Hey," she said. "That thing's here."

Elton got up from the kitchen table. He was holding a piece of buttered toast which he kept on eating as he stood beside her at the window. "Good," he said with a mouthful of crunch.

"What do you mean *good*? I told you I didn't want it."

"We made a promise."

The cat sauntered toward the field. It got smaller and smaller, until Marisol couldn't see it anymore.

"I'll get cat food today when I go into town for batteries," he said. The hands of the old clock on the kitchen wall had frozen in place. "Wanna come with me?"

Marisol shook her head. She didn't know why he kept asking.

When Elton left in the old red truck the widow had left with the house—along with a mustard-yellow tractor and enough tools to melt and start an iron factory—Marisol wandered outside. She hadn't gone outside except to hose down a few dirty plastic bins two days ago. The birds were loud, too chirpy, and Marisol squinted in the sunlight.

The cat peered out from behind a barrel.

"Hey," Marisol said.

The cat blinked at her.

"He's getting you food. In case you were wondering."

The cat did not move.

"I don't like you, either," she said. "It's fine. We'll just call it even."

The cat scampered toward the barn.

Elton was pulling on some overalls, which he had bought in town at the general store. Overalls! As if he were a farmer! As if they were going to really make this work.

"Did the widow say if that thing had a name?" Marisol asked him.

He reached for his new work boots. "Don't think so."

"That's weird," she said.

"Maybe she wanted us to name it."

"We're not naming it." She was never going to pick out names again.

"Suit yourself," he said. "Wanna come out and help me with the vegetable garden?"

She shook her head.

"Okay," he said and left her in the bedroom. Marisol was still wearing the pink terry cloth bathrobe she had brought from the city. It was just a year old, but she had worn it so much it was thinning and frayed. She wanted Elton to tell her to get dressed and go outside with him. "Do you see this day?" he used to say on Saturday mornings when they lived in the city and she was lounging around reading magazines or painting her nails. He'd point to the window. "This day is made for us. Now let's go!"

He never said that anymore. Maybe no more days were made for them.

Marisol heard Elton outside, whistling a tune she did not recognize. He'd often whistled when he was in one room and she was in another, but Marisol had always known the songs before.

She took off the robe and found some yoga pants and a sweatshirt. She didn't think people really wore these things to plant vegetables, but Marisol didn't do yoga anymore, and anyway, it's what she had.

"Now here are the seeds," he said, showing her a Seed Savers Exchange packet. "The guy at the store said these are the best for heirlooms."

She felt queasy as he ripped it open, as he poured a few into her hand. "Here's how we're going to do it," he explained. He was doing some square foot gardening thing, some technique someone at the general store had recommended since they were new to all this. Well, *he* was new. She was just witnessing.

"It's hot out here," she said.

"Go get a hat."

"I don't want a hat," she said.

"Okay." The old Elton would have teased her until she put on one.

He got down on his hands and knees and started pinching seeds into the small holes he'd made.

"Is this all we're going to plant?" Marisol asked, still standing, still holding the few tiny seeds in her cupped hand.

The plot he'd prepared was maybe twenty feet by twenty. They owned acres and acres now. Was the rest of the land just going to go to waste?

"You mean are we going to grow crops?" he asked without looking up at her.

"Isn't that what you wanted? Isn't that why we bought this place?" The sun was singeing her face. "Or was that all just talk?"

"Don't," he said, picking up the spade and spreading soil over the seeds he'd laid in the ground. "If you're not up for it, that's fine, but don't come swinging at me."

That night, she heard the cries of a baby. Marisol sat up in bed. "What's that?"

Elton didn't turn toward her. "Just the cat," he said, adjusting his pillow.

"Can you make it stop?"

"Go back to sleep," he said.

The cat showed up on the porch steps one June morning. Marisol was trying on some garden clogs Elton had bought her a few days before. Purple, chunky, plastic things. Elton had just driven off in his red truck to buy some more fertilizer at the general store, and Marisol was sitting in the porch on one of the wicker chairs the widow had left them. Chairs with worn seat cushions, green and faded and flat.

The cat swished its tail.

"I'm not letting you in the house," Marisol said through the screen door.

The cat blinked at her. It meowed once.

"I'll let you in the porch, but only for a few minutes." She unlatched the screen door.

The cat jumped up onto the one wicker rocker and curled up on the pillow.

"Figures," Marisol said. "You would take the best seat in this place."

Elton fed the cat on the porch throughout summer, and he bought it a yellow bed that he placed in the corner.

"You know what you're doing, right?" Marisol said. "It's not good."

"You started it," he said with a smile. Marisol had not seen him smile in so long that she had forgotten how it could appear when she least expected it.

Elton watered the garden. He watched for pests. He plucked worms off leaves. Some things grew—the kale took off—but the tomatoes curled up with blight.

In the extra-bedroom-turned-office, Marisol watched him out the window from her makeshift desk—an old door on two filing cabinets. She was supposed to be working. His overalls were smeared with dirt—so much dirt, so many stains, that they would never be clean again, no matter how hard she tried.

By late October, the forecast called for the first frost.

"Think we should bring the bed in for Ace?" he asked.

Ace was what he had named the cat. A female cat, they now knew after Elton had taken her to the vet. She had gotten into a fight, and her ears had required stitches.

"I said no cat in the house."

"You're right," he said. "There's always the barn."

Elton was working at the general store now. He talked about his colleagues, the advice they gave on planting, cooking, keeping out foxes when he got chickens.

"We're getting chickens?"

"Of course," Elton said. "That was always the plan."

The first evening the frost pricked the farm with cold, Marisol brought the yellow bed into the kitchen, and placed it by the pantry door. It was in the way of foot traffic, but would be there only one night. Marisol left the doors cracked so a small thing could nudge its way in. Ace did, just before nine. Marisol shut the doors, turned off lights, went upstairs.

The yellow bed stayed in the kitchen through Thanksgiving and Christmas. Marisol and Elton learned to step over it, and after a while, they stopped noticing it at all.

One January night, Marisol heard a rustling in the basement. "Ace?" she called out at the top of the stairs. The cat was always going down into the damp, dark bowels of the house when Marisol used the washer and dryer.

"Ace? Stop it, whatever you're doing," she said into the darkness. The rustling continued.

"Let it go," Elton said from the living room. He was reading the Sunday paper.

The kitchen walls were now a baby blue. Elton had gotten around to painting them over the holidays. He had also replaced the old brown stove, and Marisol stopped burning things. She wanted to blame the brown stove for all the black pancakes and charcoaled chicken, but the truth was she had learned how to not neglect something over fire.

Marisol poured water into the tea kettle and flicked on the burner. The clock on the wall ticked forward.

Ace nudged open the basement door, ambled over to Marisol and dropped something at her feet.

"What is that?" She leaned over.

A tiny mouse, grey and bloody and still. Marisol inhaled sharply but didn't move. Ace's tail swished. She sauntered away.

"Everything okay?" Elton called from the living room.

"Everything's fine," Marisol said.

With her bare hand, she picked up the mouse by the tail. Its limp and lifeless body dangled in the pinch of her fingers.

She strode through the kitchen and opened the door to the porch, and then the door to outside—to the acres they owned, to the ancient barn, to the vast darkness.

Marisol flung this small death toward the plain and waiting sky.

A Series of Pains to the Chest

Wendy BooydeGraaff

Your heart face, two floors up, framed by a small square of glass looking down on us as we walk away. My eyes swim rheumy. I can't tell by the shape of your face if you are crying or happy. It should be raining but the sky sings lakeside blue.

Smudge

Alec Kissoondyal

The baby bird crunched underfoot like freshly fallen snow. It seemed out of place beneath the brutally hot sun, amid the droplets of coagulated blood.

The tabby cat had padded down the sidewalk and dropped the blind, featherless thing, leaving it to wither on the concrete. Dennis knew it was beyond saving before he stooped for a better look. Its skin was punctured by the cat's teeth, its beak gaped open as though screaming, though no sound came.

He kept his foot firmly planted until he was sure it was enough. He stepped back, stared at the pulpy smudge that used to be a bird, then turned and walked past a group of middle-aged women whose hands were clamped over their O-shaped mouths.

Dennis felt their eyes on the back of his neck, but the sudden pain in his fingers bothered him more. He looked down and realized his cigarette had burned down to the filter, which was pinched between his thumb and forefinger. Cursing, he dropped it onto the sidewalk.

He'd given up smoking for almost a year but picked up the habit again a few months ago. Now he felt naked whenever he wasn't holding a Marlboro.

His foot hovered over the smoldering remains. He thought of the bird again and wondered if he stepped on it out of mercy, or from the same repulsion that caused the women to cover their mouths. He snuffed the embers with the heel of his shoe, then lit another cigarette and walked on.

The afternoon heat clawed at Dennis, and the familiar itch of early sunburn spread across the back of his neck. He passed diners, gas stations, and corner stores on the long trek back to his apartment. He finished the Marlboro and reached for another.

He was on his seventh cigarette by the time he reached the building, a generic red brick monstrosity with seven floors and thin walls. He stared up at the ugly, weather-stained monolith and smoked in the heat until he nearly singed his fingers again. He dropped the cigarette butt onto the concrete, completing the cancerous breadcrumb trail he'd left in his wake. He stood there, trying to think of a reason not to go in, but none came. He hurried inside before he could talk himself out of it.

A working air conditioner was not among the old building's charms. The ever-present heat followed Dennis across the threshold. He stepped into the elevator and pressed the button for the fifth floor, slumping against the wall, shifting uncomfortably in his sweat-soaked clothes.

The elevator chimed. Dennis peeled himself off the wall and trudged down the hallway to his apartment. The feeling of trepidation returned; he felt it roiling in his belly and pulsating in the roots of his teeth. Once again, he acted before he could think twice and unlocked the door.

She was standing on the balcony. Her copper hair trailed limply down her back. The door was open. He called her name.

"Angela."

She remained still, then slowly turned and walked inside. She wore a black t-shirt and blue jeans. She wasn't sweating despite the heat. She never did. He used to tease her and say it was her superpower. He felt envious; his shirt was so thoroughly soaked, it had become translucent.

"How was your walk?" she asked, forcing a smile.

"Fine." Silence followed.

They stood there awkwardly in the living room. It was empty except for the cardboard boxes piled in the corner. Angela sniffed the air.

"You don't have to avoid smoking around me anymore," she said.

"It just doesn't feel right."

"I thought you wanted to quit."

"I don't have a reason to anymore."

Angela's smile wavered. She brushed a loose strand of hair away from her face.

"How's the view?" He asked.

"I'm going to miss it."

Dennis glanced at the boxes. "Is that the last of them?"

Angela nodded. "Yeah, all packed and ready to go. We can go ahead and load them in my car."

"How do you like your new place?"

"It's fine," she looked over her shoulder at the balcony. "The view isn't as good as here, though."

"It never seemed like much of a view to me."

She shrugged. "It puts things into perspective."

"Does it give you hope for the future?"

"It helps me cope with the present," she said. "How about you? Have your walks been helping?"

"Sometimes," Dennis replied. "Most days, I just need an excuse to get out of this damn place."

"Well, you won't have to come back after today."

"Yeah," he said. "We should probably start moving those boxes."

Dennis heard her sigh as he turned. He looked back at her.

"What is it?'

"I didn't say anything."

"But you want to," Dennis insisted. The fresh ravages of sunburn raked at his nerves. "Come on, just say it."

She bit her lower lip, as she often did when she was thinking. Her teeth stood out against the wine-dark red of her lipstick. "How long are you going to keep avoiding it?"

"I don't even know what the hell you mean."

"You know exactly what I mean." Angela tried to keep the frustration out of her voice, but Dennis had known her long enough to hear it creep in. "Come on, it's been nearly three months, and you've barely said a word about it."

"Right," Dennis spat back. He slapped the box on the top of the stack; his singed fingers throbbed faintly. "You sure picked a hell of a time to talk about it."

"I've tried before," Angela reminded him. "But every time I bring it up, it just leads to another argument, and you storm out on one of your *walks*!"

"I told you already, sometimes I just need to get the hell away from here!"

"Away from me, you mean."

"Jesus Christ." Dennis kneaded the bridge of his nose with his sore fingers. "Don't act like you're any different. You stand out on that fucking balcony all day. Then you come in here and talk about how it gives you *perspective* and helps you *cope*, but we both know that's bullshit!"

"You know what *really* helps me cope when I go out there?" Angela's voice was barely a whisper; she never yelled when she was truly angry.

"No, I don't know. Why don't you fucking tell me already?"

"I look down and tell myself that I could jump if I wanted to, and if I made myself fall just right, it would be all over, even if I'm only five floors up. Every day I think about doing it, and every day I step away. If I don't, who would be left to remember him?"

"I would," Dennis said shakily. His arms bristled with goosebumps despite the heat. "I think about him every day."

Angela shook her head. "No, you spend all day trying to forget him. You think the hurt will just go away one day if you try hard enough, but it won't. We may be going our separate ways, but all the shit that's happened will always be a part of both of us, no matter how hard you try to ignore it."

"You have no fucking clue," Dennis said through clenched teeth. Angela's face blurred as tears clouded his vision.

She folded her arms across her chest. "Try me."

"You felt all the right things, all the things you were supposed to feel. As a mother. As a decent fucking human being! You were so beside yourself, they had to sedate you. You know the first thing I felt when I saw him wasting away like some fucking science experiment in the NICU?" Tears burned his cheeks. "Relief! Part of me was actually *glad* that it happened, can you believe that? For a second, I thought everything would go back to normal. I wouldn't have an extra mouth to feed, I wouldn't have to throw away my dreams, I wouldn't have to learn how to be a . . . I just . . . Everything reminds me of him. It's not just this apartment, it's not just you. It's everything. No matter where I go, no matter what I do, I *can't fucking escape it*!"

A cocktail of emotions surged through his veins as he shouted the final words. It was the same powder keg of rage, sorrow, disgust, and helplessness that gave him the fortitude to snuff baby birds like cigarette butts. He grabbed the box on the top of the pile with both hands and hurled it across the room.

It crashed against the wall and fell sideways onto the floor. The cardboard flaps sprang open, scattering the contents across the carpet: a few books, some t-shirts, rolled up movie posters—and a teddy bear with a blue ribbon around its neck. It stared at Dennis with coal-black button eyes.

"I thought we got rid of everything," Dennis said as he stared back.

"I couldn't part with it," Angela said quietly. "It helps me remember him."

Dennis's eyes lingered on the bear, but his mind drifted elsewhere.

He remembered the way Angela looked when they first met. She stood tall and proud, drenched in the red and blue sheen of the bar's neon lights, like a warrior queen smeared with the psychedelic blood of some slain pagan war god.

They made love that same night, but he barely remembered it. The months that followed killed anything pleasant about their first meeting. The mood was as blue as the ribbon on the bear and the two lines on the pregnancy test.

Where would they live, how would they take care of a child? It wasn't right to bring another life into a world full of children who were already suffering. But in the end, that was exactly what they decided to do.

They moved in together, on the fifth floor with the balcony. Slowly but surely life seemed to get better, and by the time they found out that they would be having a boy, blue didn't seem like such a bad color after all, and nine months didn't seem like such a long time.

Angela's water broke in six.

The entire day was still vivid in Dennis's mind, but the thing he remembered most was the tiny, pallid, breathless boy, who withered under the hospital's fluorescent lights, just like . . .

"Hey," Angela said. "Dennis? Are you OK?"

"Fuck," Dennis said, horrified. "I don't know why I get like this, I really—"

He let out a choked sob before he could finish. He stood there crying in the middle of the sweltering room, surrounded by the mess he'd made. It was what he seemed to do best these days.

Then, he saw a flash movement through the tears and felt a familiar coolness as Angela wrapped her arms around him. She pressed her face against his shoulder, and he felt a fresh dampness seep into the fabric of his shirt. He hugged her back. They sank to their knees in each other's arms, wracked with sobs that made their bodies shudder.

None of it mattered. Not the mess, not the heat, not the women with their O-shaped mouths, not even the balcony or the baby bird.

"I'm so sorry," he sobbed.

"It's alright," she whispered. "I understand."

When they finally calmed down enough to let go of one another, Dennis dragged himself over to the box and flipped it upright. "Guess we should clean all this up, huh?"

Angela wiped the tears from her eyes and nodded.

They crawled across the floor, grabbing whatever was in arm's reach until the only thing that remained was the bear. Dennis reached for it, but Angela gently grabbed his wrist before he could pick it up.

"Don't put it back," Angela said. "I want you to have it."

"I can't," Dennis said.

"I don't need it anymore," she said. "I can practically see him on the back of my eyelids."

"Are you sure?"

She released his wrist.

"Thank you, Angela."

"Come on," she said. "We really should get all this stuff downstairs."

It didn't take them long to pack everything into the trunk of the beat-up grey Toyota, but the heat made it harder than it should have been. Even Angela was sweating.

"You losing your powers?" Dennis teased. A stray lock of hair had plastered itself against her forehead, and he brushed it aside. "Is exercise your kryptonite or something?"

She playfully swatted his hand away. "Fuck you."

They laughed for a while and savored the silence that came after.

"Well," Dennis said after a moment, "it was fun while it lasted."

"No, it wasn't." She smiled and kissed his cheek.

After she drove away, Dennis went back to the apartment and stood in the living room until he heard the shrill ring of silence in the hot, stagnant air. The bear was the only thing that remained. It sat in the corner of the living room where he'd left it.

"Looks like it's just us now," he said, stooping to pick it up. He cradled it in his arms as he walked onto the balcony.

He looked out at the single-story buildings that shimmered in the heat, then at the concrete directly below, and thought of what Angela had said. He touched the spot on his cheek where she'd kissed him. He felt the residual stickiness that the smudge of lipstick had left on his face, and remembered how her skin was as cold as freshly fallen snow.

Elegy for the dead cat on the side of Mopac

Rae Rozman

Blue collar silver bell/must have been somebody's baby/far from home and alone that's the way I'll probably die too/ Russian blue/the way Katya said kot like it was a pet name for everyone/and she has a baby now—Katya, not the cat/ though somebody may have called you baby, kot/and here we are alone in a moment we pretend not to see/is it heartbreak if it's not your heart that broke/listen, kot, do you hear the requiem playing low and slow/stalking death across four lanes of traffic/her voice a silver bell/calling you home

Carlos

E.H. Cowles

a lizard trapped inside my house
crawls across a carpet desert
in my sunroom
where it cannot find food or water
outside flies buzz against the window
and grass glistens with dew

I want to travel before I get too old to move
I have seen it among the migratory species
an old buffalo left behind
when the herd moves south on the cusp of winter
I am not thinking about my feet
it is the Nissan frontier
with a fiberglass topper
and a futon mattress in the truck bed
a reincarnation of that VW mini-bus
decorated in paisley Zoroastrian symbols
of life and eternity
with peace signs painted on its doors
it seems like a long time ago
when we traveled the beatnik road
from Coney Island to San Francisco

in that summer of love
we believed in freedom and self-determination
for all of humankind
we became consciously suspicious of government actions
we rejected consumerism and capitalist values
we embraced free-love and feminism
we opposed the Vietnam war and
protested nuclear armament
we marched to end segregation

the lizard is entangled in carpet fuzz
a few feet from the narrow threshold space under the door
that delineates the border between life and death

I read stories about immigrants suffocating in 18-wheelers
I have seen the photograph
of a dead man on the river bank
I have seen the faces of children
crying for their mothers
I have witnessed
human lives treated like commodities
in an ecosystem nourished by desperation

I give the lizard a name handed down
by a conquistador
who once stood awestruck
upon the steps of a Mayan temple
Carlos

I understand Carlos
you will not survive without my help
I am a benevolent coyote
there is no human trafficking cartel threatening your life
Carlos
there is no candlelit altar in the hallway of my house
decorated with statues of the skinny woman
lady of shadows
la Santa Muerte
Carlos
I untangle the lizard from the carpet fuzz
lift it up gently between my fingers
open the door to the outside
and drop the lizard
into a gardenia bush

Cora Speaks to Objects

Rebecca Anderson

Everything is sentient. Just not everyone can see, hear, and feel the life that pulsates through dining room chairs, lamps, cell phones, and the detritus of consumerism. All of it lives an inner life as rich as our own.

I remember noticing this for the first time when I was young, maybe three or four, when a lightbulb blew. My family heard a pop and sighed with annoyance as our living room darkened. I heard a literal goodbye, punctuated by a satisfied laugh. It was a wistful farewell: "See you on the other side, Cora," he said, vanishing into blankness.

I should have known it would be too coincidental that I had this gift. Our family was in the antiques business—it had been our tradition for three generations: to collect and covet objects and, quite literally, put them on a pedestal just for being.

The night before I was born, dad got drunk and took a baseball bat to the shop. That was the catalyst for me being born, in fact. My mother, in her sadness and rage, began to contract, bleeding out on the oriental rugs that must have cringed at the brown-crimson stains on the white fringe, after a hundred-plus years of maintaining the vivid color of their youth.

My great-aunt Rose, a doula who had birthed my mother, aunts and uncles, and countless other family members, shook her head with sadness when she saw the mess that was our family store. She was the family matriarch. A recluse and a shaman who could heal any ailment. "They'll never appreciate being guardians of the objects, but you will," she muttered under her breath before kissing my forehead. "More than all of us."

You're never alone when everything around you speaks and you're the only one who can hear. That felt like chaos when I was a child in school. The chipper chatter of my teacher's chalk as it faded to dust. Agonized wails when the bad boys carved their names into the surfaces of wooden desks.

Attention Deficit Disorder, the teachers and therapists first called it, after they noticed me entranced by the colorful classroom posters (they told great jokes) or the brass apple on my teacher's desk who introduced me to the ideas of irony and cynicism.

Schizophrenia, they later called it, after which they filled me full of medications and hospitalized me in a place where the blue cotton blankets were bitter and rude, and the clock on the wall—encased by a screen to stop us from breaking its glass and using it as a weapon—showed signs of depression himself.

The drugs didn't work because you can't medicate away reality. And that's what I saw: reality beyond what others were capable of perceiving. I knew it wasn't a mental illness. My parents knew too, but they couldn't decide what was harder to accept: a child who was psychotic or one who possessed a magical gift.

My father didn't see it as a gift, though. "A damn curse," I heard him tell my mother one night after he thought I was in bed. I was 15, and had just gotten home from my third psychiatric hospitalization. "I know it was *that witch Rose.* She cursed Cora. I know it."

Mother stared at him for a moment in silence. "Maybe I should talk to her."

I'm not sure she ever did.

When I was 25, I fell in love with a 19th century armchair. An old family friend, I suppose you could have called him. Sam is what he went by. At that point, my parents had all but retired, leaving me to run the store by myself. Sam and I had all the time in the world together, and I spent much of it letting his worn, green velvet envelop my body. It was sensual. I gently stroked his mahogany arm and he told me stories about his early days in Victorian London and a ship ride to New York after his first family discarded him at auction. He knew my grandparents. "They were like you," he finally told me after a year into our relationship.

"*Passionate* about antiques," I giggled, running my finger across his ornately carved back.

"Actually, yes."

"Really?"

"Really."

"Could . . . they hear you? Talk to you?"

"Every day, all day."

"Animism," said Aunt Rose, before I could get out the words of my question. "Your great-grandparents, my mother and father, they had it too."

"Animism . . . " I savored the word I wish I had known decades before.

Aunt Rose squeezed my hand. "It's just the underlying way of the world: Everything has a soul and a perspective as rich as our own. Just not everyone can see it."

"Can you?"

"No, but I have other gifts. We're only given the abilities we need, Cora."

"And I needed this?" I was in love with someone who everyone else saw as a chair, a hundred years my elder.

"You did. Every object in that store did. They needed respect and true love."

My parents asked me to step back from the antique business when I priced everything in the store—each individual object—at a million dollars because I couldn't bear to let my friends go. I had stopped mentioning my gift to my parents, but they began to suspect mental illness (hoarding this time), when I held onto each object that passed through the door.

"Cora, I get that you care—" Mother started.

"You'll run us out of business," Father interjected. "We can't afford to do this."

Unfortunately, Sam agreed. "It's the way of the world."

I stared at him silently. Sometimes I resented his wisdom.

"We live in a world of commerce and impermanence," he continued. "We can love and cherish things—especially us objects—but none of us can possess something, someone, forever."

"That's bullshit!" Tears welled in my eyes. "You're almost 130 years old! What's stopping me from holding onto you until my time on earth is gone?"

"Well, nothing, but that's not my point."

"Then what is?"

"You'll have to learn that for yourself, I suppose."

I was mad at Sam. Maybe objects didn't love the way we did; maybe their "soul" that Aunt Rose spoke of was limited. I flitted around the store cutting down prices of pieces I could bear to lose: the tea set with the annoying voice, the table that prattled on with his dated viewpoints, and—although it saddened me—the quiet curio cabinet I was just getting to know.

"Are you happy now?" I asked Sam, dropping heavily into his seat after turning over the ticklish 'closed' sign in the front window.

"Why would I be, Cora?"

"Because I listened to you. I marked things down. I agreed to let them go."

"I still don't think you understand what I was trying to tell you."

I kept my mouth shut because I just wanted to feel close to Sam. I spent the night in the shop, stroking his fabric gently as I drifted to sleep.

Mother came in early the next morning and urged me to go home, shower, and take the day off. I felt light and hopeful, so against my usual impulses to stay as close as possible to Sam, I left. After a hot shower, I put on the vintage dress that boosted my ego but knew how to stay quiet and returned to the store to settle in for the evening. My mother was nowhere to be seen.

"Sam!" I called out.

There was no reply.

"Sammy?"

He wasn't in his usual place at the back of the store. My stomach dropped.

"Is something wrong, sweetheart?" My mother emerged from the office.

"That chair. The old green one. My . . . chair." Something was wrong.

"I sold it."

I thought my mother was joking. She had to be. There's no way she would have done that. Not that she knew how I felt about him, but he had been in our family for generations.

"Actually, I gave it away for free." Mother smiled, as though this was something to be proud of. "It was too worn to sell, and this sweet old lady, God bless her . . . ."

My legs gave out and I crumpled to the floor.

"Cora, what's wrong?" She had no idea the damage she had done.

"He was my whole world." I sobbed so hard Mother could barely make out my words

"Who was?"

"Sam."

"I don't know who Sam is, honey . . . ."

I crawled to my feet and straightened my dress, who tried to shush me to no avail.

"You wouldn't, Mother." My eyes locked hers and I felt nothing but hatred. My human family didn't get me. Aunt Rose was right: I was given the gifts I needed, the gift of finding my place in a world that couldn't see or hear.

"Cora . . . ."

"Who did you give the chair to?"

"What does it matter? Let it go."

I stood inches from her face. She wasn't family to me at that moment. "I'll ask you again: Who did you give the chair to?"

"This is absurd." Mother paused. "It was an elderly woman. I think she was homeless, if you must know. I'm sure she'd appreciate that nasty old thing."

Homeless. My Sam would be living on the streets.

"How did a *homeless* woman get an armchair out of here?"

Mother shrugged. "She dragged it out."

If she took him on foot, she couldn't have gotten far. I turned and ran out the door. I could find him and reclaim what was mine.

The afternoon was rainy, but I walked the streets, down back alleys and behind dumpsters who told me they hadn't seen an elderly woman with an antique green armchair. I creeped into empty warehouses and walked along the highway, near the empty fields littered with trash, to tent cities filled with sad nylon domes that yearned for days at Boy Scout campouts and family vacations long forgotten. Still, I couldn't find Sam.

I searched every day, sunup to sundown, expanding my radius and getting bolder. I went into abandoned houses and talked to angry sofas that had been eaten by mice. I began to talk to humans, even. "Have you seen a green chair?" I'd ask. They'd look confused. "An antique one, with mahogany arms and the most gorgeous Victorian filigree carvings on the back?" I began to add that he was mine, *stolen.*

I started to get some leads. They'd seen him with a woman who lived under an overpass not too far away.

It was dark by the time I got there, my heart pounding with anticipation.

Through the light of a small campfire, I saw him.

A woman sat on his lap, her matted hair pressed against his back and her legs curled up on him the way I used to. I cried out in horror.

"What the hell do you want?" the woman slurred.

"Cora!" Sam sounded surprised. The woman couldn't hear him.

"Ma'am that's . . . my chair."

"Cora, don't do this . . . ." I heard the sadness in Sam's voice.

"Fuck off," the woman said.

I ignored her.

"Sam, I'm going to bring you home."

"I'm not fucking Sam," the woman stood up and moved toward me. I backed up, falling hard to the ground.

"Cora, go home," Sam implored.

"You don't love me . . ." I wanted to run away, but I couldn't pick myself up. "Did you ever . . . .?"

"Let me stay. I'm the only comfort she has," Sam pleaded.

I didn't want to hear it. I didn't want to accept that it might be true.

The woman stared down at me with a look of pity, and I glared into her dirt-streaked face, trying to muster up rage. She took from me the only being who gave my life meaning.

I crawled away with heaving sobs. Sam didn't bother to bid me farewell.

A decanter shaped like a pheasant showed interest in me. I agreed to a date, mostly out of boredom. He was banal. Created in the 1970s, he had spent most of his life on the dusty shelf of a family who sold him at a yard sale for fifty cents. It was a sad story, but I couldn't muster up any real sympathy.

It had been six months since I last saw Sam.

After the night I discovered him under the overpass, I drove by a few times just to make sure he was okay. He sat there, waterlogged and filthy, but always with his new *friend? owner?* close by.

I was depressed, which worried my parents. Father tried to set me up on a date with a human, but I couldn't imagine that working. Mother called Aunt Rose, who came to the shop and held my hand as I sat heartbroken on a broken particle board bench who understood what it meant to feel worthless and discarded.

"You're the guardian of this place, Cora," Aunt Rose reminded me as I told her about Sam. "That's why you have this gift, to carry on the family legacy. It's bigger than just one chair."

"But I loved him."

"And you always will, I'm sure." She paused. "It's the same with us regular folks, too, you know. We love and we lose, but we can never fully possess another being."

I listened quietly.

"The difference between you and the rest of us?" Aunt Rose added, "We have seven billion people in the world to choose from when it comes to love. Your choices are infinite."

When Aunt Rose left, I walked around the store, greeting the objects I'd long taken for granted. Still lonely, I stared at the door to the attic. How long had it been since I'd been up there? Ten years? Fifteen? We didn't collect enough new objects to need it for storage these days, so it had been untouched for a while.

I climbed the stairs, into a dusty room filled with sleepy grandfather clocks and chipper divans. Nothing interesting. As I turned to head back downstairs, a table in the corner of the room caught my eye. Mahogany, with ornate legs carved in a familiar pattern that made my heart pound.

"Hello." I greeted the table shyly.

"Hi there, pretty girl. It's been a long time since anyone's been up here."

I reached out and brushed the dust off his surface and he let out a satisfied sigh.

"I'm Cora, by the way."

"Max."

"Hey Max, would you mind if I take you downstairs?"

"Sure, whatever you'd like." He reminded me so much of Sam.

"I have a great shop. I think we could find someone to buy you in no time."

The Landscape Listens

Holly M. Hofer

These weeds toy with my roses
and mosey corrosive behind my eyes.

There are censors but they are drowning in the fishpond
catching me catching this mood catching

the cardinal from my birdhouse   wings
        into oblivion

Stuck down (gravity and old tennis shoes), I am quick to judge. *Arrogant*: to fly.

A sore   with round,
      -colored bug   black bruises,
                                                    crawls up   to escape
                                                                my sleeve   the brightening

        sun.

I was young and thought myself perfectly lucky to encounter little ladies, bright.
I placed one on the tip of my finger
and she chose to fly about her manor of roses and green under the sun—

there is no time for this

(something supposed is settling in my eye)

—

Why, I am afraid again.

Has someone slipped a secret tangle in?

The fish can see it, their goggle-eyes
catching   me   catching   it   catching

the weed's roots are long,
and the ladybug still hides in the dark.
So snooty, the brown bird, alighting always atop the highest limb.

I whisper to my roses that we will never fly again,
never fly. *We never did*, the flowers soothe,
we never did fly.

Little Bird

Adam Knight

I still think of the awful noise, though I neither saw nor heard it. The sound was probably a tiny splat, the blast a quick, squelchy spray. But my mind imagines a blast of sound and gore that makes my throat tighten, even twenty years later. What haunts me is the laughter. Two adolescent chuckles that, as they echo across decades, have become the sound of senseless violence.

The air that morning was warm and fresh. It had rained the night before, but now on Saturday morning the sky was blue and clear, the June sun causing a little steam to rise from the grass of the baseball field. My team arrived for a 9 A.M. game, then sat in the dugouts, waiting to see if the muddy puddles would evaporate enough for us to take the field.

I sat on the wooden bench, gazing out through the chain link fence. I had always loved playing baseball. But now I was thirteen, and this year, games brought both excitement and dread. My position was reserve right fielder; in other words, I was terrible. I was the player the coaches put in the field for the fewest required innings, in the least stressful position. At the plate, I could anticipate a box score of 0 for 3 with 2 strikeouts and 1 groundout. Maybe, if I kept the bat on my shoulders and the opposing pitcher was errant enough, I could take a walk. This was the way I scored my only run of the season: by walking, and then two batters later, our Ajax of a first baseman hit a homerun to right center. In the words of my teammates, he "parked it." No one told me I was bad, but I knew it. So I sat on the bench, watching the puddles not dry, feeling disappointment and relief that we wouldn't be playing.

As a lumbering twelve-year-old, I had loved Little League. Tryouts were generous. Practices were unstrenuous. Games ended in pizza and sno-cones at the concession stand, double treats for the winning team. But at age thirteen, I joined Senior League, where in practice we played catch barehanded and did a running drill called "suicides." The part of games I dreaded most was the warmup lap around the outfield fence. The best runners on the team would have returned to the dugout, their heart rates barely elevated, as I gasped and trudged my way across the vast expanse of center field. In Little League, playing for fun had been enough. In Senior League, it was not.

A metallic rattle clanged in the air. I looked up. One of my teammates, Nick, was pacing back and forth, dragging his aluminum bat along the chain link fence.

"C'mon," he moaned. "It's not so bad. Let's just play."

Our coach shrugged.

"Not my call, boys. Umps decide."

"This is bullshit," Nick said. I wasn't so sure.

"It's just mud," said Scott, another teammate. Nick and Scott were best friends, and like me, were thirteen. Unlike me, they were very good ballplayers. Nick was a small, wiry slap hitter who could turn singles into doubles. His father owned our town's biggest car dealership. Scott was tall and broad, a big bruiser of a kid who had set records crushing homeruns his last year of Little League. He had gained infamy in sixth grade by tasting a piece of the cow heart we were dissecting in science class. Today, he's a cop.

A fluttering movement caught my eye. I looked down. What I had mistaken for some windblown leaves was a bird's nest, probably knocked from the dugout roof in the previous night's storm. In it lay a baby bird with a bulbous head and wispy feathers. Its beak opened and shut, emitting the tiniest "cheep" that was only audible in the gaps of teenage conversation.

Hello, I thought. *Hello, there.*

The baby bird looked up at me. At least I thought he did. He flapped a broken wing.

Cheep cheep cheep.

A lot of people were walking around the dugout and no one had noticed the fallen nest. I felt an urge to scoop it up in my hands. But what was I going to do? Hold on to it? Give it my seat on the bench? Buy it a sno-cone at the concession stand? My hands went still.

"This blows," declared Nick, pacing again. That bat, rattling the cage. "Just mud. What kind of pussies won't let us play with mud on the field?"

I did not say that I thought playing with puddles in the field would probably result in torn ligaments and bone bruises. If I did say something, I would be a pussy.

"Aren't there buckets or mops or something to dry the field?" asked Scott.

"The field was built this way," the coach explained. "They constructed it on a layer of clay for whatever reason. Now it doesn't drain. We have to wait and see if the sun will dry it before they have to call the game."

"Think it'll happen?" asked another teammate.

"Probably not," the coach replied.

"Goddammit," Nick said. Then he resumed dragging the bat and rattling the cage.

Nick did not see the nest as he stepped closer to it. I thought to call out to him, or to lunge forward and protect the bird. But I did not. I cringed. And Nick's foot passed over the nest, clearing it by inches. Still, he did not see it.

I asked myself what I'd even do if I picked up the nest. I wasn't a veterinarian, nor did I think one could help. A baby bird with no mother and no flight? It would never survive. Yet I could not stop sneaking glances at the fragile body, nor could I shut out the repetitive *cheep cheep cheep,* so high and thin that only I could hear it.

Time passed, the minutes unspooling in exquisite torture. Umpires and coaches conferred. The players speculated, or complained, or joked about girls in class. I thought about saving an injured baby bird. The coach returned.

"They'll give it ten more minutes, but it looks like they'll call the game."

Now Nick stomped up and down the dugout. I could read on the coach's face that he wanted to tell Nick to cool it. But he didn't and wouldn't say anything. Nick's father had sold cars to half the people in town. No one told his son to cool it.

Cheep cheep cheep. Cheep cheep cheep.

I felt like the bird and I were in a little, private world. He was my secret. I did not know if could help him, but I could listen to him. *You are not alone,* I thought. I imagined what it must be like to be the bird, a tiny waif, perhaps days old, disoriented and scared, flailing and crying in a world full of creatures much larger and louder than he. *I hear you, little bird. I see you.*

In the next ten minutes, my bravery built. A plan started to form in my mind. The game would be postponed; that was apparent. I would be going home in fifteen minutes. I could wait after everyone left the dugout, then feigning having forgotten something, go back in. I looked at my glove. Folded over, I could hide the nest so no one could see me sneak it out. What would happen next, I had no idea. But at least, if I could get the nest out of the dugout . . . .

The umps called the game. In a flurry of scraping cleats and teenage grumbles, our team packed its belongings and prepared to go home. I collected my hat, bat, and glove, all while keeping a glancing eye on the little bird. *I'm coming back for you,* I thought. *Two minutes.*

We filed out of the dugout. I tried to exude nonchalance.

I walked toward my waiting parents. I had rehearsed this in my mind. Wait until everyone was gone from the dugout, announce aloud that I had forgotten something, then turn around, get the nest, and get out.

"Hey Nick! Check this out!" Scott called. I froze.

A few seconds later, Nick and Scott strolled out of the dugout. Nick held the nest in his hands. He held it out to show anyone who would see.

"What do you want to do with it?" Scott asked.

"Let's take it up to the high school field and park it!"

And then they laughed.

I am tempted to write that their laughter was cruel, full of the vinegar of malice. But it wasn't. It was the laughter of late childhood, two boys getting ready for some good, clean fun. Rollerblading, ice cream-eating, mini-golfing, baby bird-bashing fun.

I had one last opportunity. Face up to Nick and Scott, demand they give me the nest. But of course I did not. I got in the car with my parents, and said nothing.

All day at home, I was morose and quiet. My imagination commandeered my thoughts, and I was troubled by an incessant *cheep cheep cheep,* cut off in a blast of blood and shattered bones. Over and over, I imagined Nick and Scott at the high school field, taking the fateful, fatal swing. I wondered which one would do it. No doubt, they would both be laughing.

I had lunch. I had dinner. I went through my day, my mind imprisoned by my secret. Finally, that night, my mom came to say goodnight. She asked me what was wrong. I cried. I sobbed and told her the story in gasping breaths. She hugged me and reassured me of how good and sweet and caring I was. She said that what Nick and Scott did was cruel and mean and I was nothing like them. *No kidding,* I thought.

Something died that day. Not just a newly hatched sparrow on a high school baseball field, but also something in me. As a boy, I had played baseball on a team with other boys, and though we may have all had different temperaments, we all could play the game we loved. But that morning's events confirmed for me finally that I did not belong. Not on the team and not with other guys. My path to manhood, whatever it might look like, would not look like Nick and Scott's. Their path was paved with death, their camaraderie forged in cruelty. My path was paved in cowardice, and my solitude forged in compassion. Still, many years later, I can hear the *cheep cheep cheep cheep cheep cheep* of a helpless voice, cut short because I was too fearful of being mocked. Nick and Scott did not kill that bird alone. My silence was their accomplice.

Sightseeing

M. Cynthia Cheung

It was 3 P.M. our last day in Iceland, and sunset
was nine hours away. We parked along the highway, listening
to the car's ticking, the wind's mutter over the lava field.

Through the scoria we walked—until finally, half-disbelieving,
we arrived at the head of a track beside a low stone wall.
It was as if I could see the Vikings of mythology,

Halli and Leiknir, their thick-boned hands again clearing the path,
hefting moss-riddled boulders. You nodded: *Yes, I see it.*
Their grave lay beyond the wall, marked

by a sign. What were we after, you and I, the heirs of refugees?
We were newly married, with a longing to trace the shape
of our descent from people—family—whose strange hand-painted

records we neither knew existed, nor could read. Yet here,
ancestors were everywhere, common as fitted stones,
or midnight dusk. Stories stacked upon earth.

How we clung to one another, two foreigners in the wilderness, turning
and turning to the ash plumes rising from the turf.

Dragon Flies

Steven Beauchamp

In late summer they appear
out of thin air cruising down the street,
veering off into this yard and that,
glinting reddish bronze in bright sunlight.
Pushing the mower in broad open spaces of my yard,
I see them hovering like an escort squadron
of biplane fighters attacking insects
flushed by wheels and whirring blade.

As a boy fishing in the creek,
sometimes one would light on the end
of my long cane pole. "Snake doctor"
the country folks called them
following some old legend or myth.

They swirl around me as I stop to mop the sweat
from my brow. Good company, this flying circus,
stitching together this moment
with boyhood and ancient past.

In darker mood, sometimes I imagine them
huge and black like shadows of vultures.
Wings swept, insistent propeller drone.
I see a grandmother in Pakistan
picking vegetables in the garden behind the house,
children playing in the front yard
when the Hellfire Missile struck.
Her body, blown to pieces, mingled
with bits of vegetables, blood with tomato juice,
eyes with chunks of eggplant,
matted hair in a nearby mango tree.

Snake master of the world uncoiling
ever in the blackening air:
Is this the medicine you bring?
From memories so deeply burned,
what lessons learned?
Mopping my brow, I push on.

Let's consider three of my students

Jeremiah O'Hagan

1. The girl with the tiny lies
   Every morning I say "good morning" even on the mornings mine sucks. I say it because maybe she needs to hear it, I think, because every time I ask her if she is in fact having a good morning, she tells me she is, when her shimmering brown eyes are as sad as the puddles on the side of the road after rains—slicked rainbows with no bottom.

2. The boy with the yellow hand
   He tells me he needs to go to the nurse to get his busted hand swabbed and re-taped. And he's so casual about it. When he comes back it nearly sparkles. Swollen, buttery skin with pin-prick bloody stars spangled across the knuckles. Band-aids cover the bare spots where he left himself on the wall. Did they x-ray the bones, find the spots where he snapped? Can x-rays go that deep?

3. The girl who falls down
   If you saw her have a seizure you might not believe she's dangerous with her words. She'll knock you down faster than you can stop her. I know, I tried one day when she was sinking against the wall, her body a ribbon of pain and fear and rebellion. I tried to catch her but she was falling all at once, the way her words hit me every time.

The Geminids

Linda McMullen

December 2: I managed to miss it yesterday, but now I find it's December again and Cass—as ever—claims my thoughts.

It began very innocently with a pair of co-workers casting about for a subject besides the oppressive news or the nearly irrelevant low-level sexual tension between them. Lowering her eyes, one mentioned that she and her daughter planned to stay up late to watch the meteor shower.

The Geminids.

Cass.

In seventh grade, we both stood five feet, two inches tall. We both had long brown hair. We both had braces. Jace, the undisputed king of our class, declared us twins. I don't think I imagined that rapid crinkle of Cass's nose. I didn't blame her, really—she and her sylvan face and form had perfected the Hollister aesthetic while my mother had me cruising the larger girls' racks at Target. I answered Ms. Warner's questions about the Golden Fleece and hid my face behind an infinity scarf. I never talked to my therapist about that, the revelatory nanosecond of manifest disdain.

December 5: Today my Facebook Memories included photos from high school graduation. Cass as valedictorian, me as salutatorian.

Sometime during spring of senior year Cass and I—sharing a slate of AP classes as well as trading off playing Viola in *Twelfth Night*—got into a heated debate during our confirmation class about St. Elmo's fire. I can't remember now who took which side. One of us argued vociferously that the Catholic Church had glommed onto ancient sailors' superstitions and reverence for the Gemini, and the other vehemently defended St. Elmo's miraculous proclivities. Cass's hair tumbled out of its deliberately messy bun, framing her heart-shaped face, now bright red. I had a *moment*, a burst of time-frozen emotion, although I couldn't tell what my hand intended as it swept toward her cheek—

Instead, I pulled back, hissed, "You'll never make it as a reporter, if you can't keep your cool during a stupid argument."

I may as well have slapped her.

December 9: Today the alumni newsletter included a lengthy article about Cass. *Article*—I say, *article*. The 'o' word sounds so final.

We both attended the State University at Midwest Falls, a respectable if not elite institution with a storied journalism program. We vied for glory at the newspaper—I earned accolades with a story about the budget office's creative accounting; she countered by gaining acclaim after exposing a history professor's neo-Nazi online tirades.

The night before the editorship was announced, we watched a lunar eclipse tinge the moon and the surrounding stars with a gory luster.

"It'll be you," she said.

"They'll have us share it," I replied.

She turned to me, her lips in a resigned pout. "I'm sure," she said, tightly, "that you deserve it."

I got the editorship. Cass announced her imminent transfer to American University's School of Communication.

I wonder: did I briefly consider chucking it all, and joining her?

December 12: I checked *Humans of New York* out of the library today. Someone had left a pair of bookmarks inside it.

Cass got into Columbia for graduate school. With a scholarship. She texted, "Just thought I'd let you know . . . ."

I opened my meager envelope as the nonentity in the dorm room next door blared Madonna's "Lucky Star."

It did not begin with the word *Congratulations.*

I swore so loudly the CD skipped.

I did get into a school. Just not *the* school. It was shortly thereafter that I took up boxing. "It's great for working off pent-up energy," I told friends. My school's coach happened to see me one day at the gym, impressed me into the team. Due to my stature, my nickname on the circuit was the Pugnacious Peanut.

December 17: Everything reminds me. Even my mother's reproofs. *Don't you want to come home? Don't you think we miss you? Do you have to be so negative?*

"Does it have to be New York?" my mother asked, when I headed east without an apartment, a job, or a plan.

I took a waitressing job and found my way into semi-legal midnight frays to make the rent. I wrote freelance.

I thought about what I wanted to do with my life.

I found a sublet. Cass had an apartment in the building opposite.

She had a real knack for rigging cold packs out of frozen pea bags, hand towels, and hair rubber bands. Sometimes, late, we decided that the other side of the street was simply too far to go.

December 22: I'm supposed to write, for my job. The cursor blinks ominously at me from the top left corner of the screen.

It came easily, once. One of my pieces—a jocular little essay about my life as a boxer of the demimonde—went viral. Creepy men and one decidedly respectable job offer at a certain well-known print publication slid into my DMs.

Cass said, "Ironic that this means the Peanut will hang up her gloves."

She never once came to see me fight.

I snorted, "Don't you have some homework to finish?"

December 24: Earlier today I walked by the church, observed the twin rows of shepherds before the nativity, kneeling before the single star.

Cass announced on Christmas Eve that she was dropping out of school. She didn't put it that way, though. She declared, *I've gotten a new job.* Atlanta. A friend of a friend from AU. International affairs. Bonuses, perks. Correspondent. The words came out in a rush, or I heard them in one. We didn't live anywhere near the subway but I had to cover my ears—the only sound was an oncoming train.

I screamed, "You can't stand that I finally made it, can you?"

December 27: That date—previously vanished in the insouciant blur between Christmas and New Year's—is tattooed on my left wrist.

That day, I switched on CNN. Waited to hear the reportage from America's longest war, to watch Cass interviewing sober government officials or Taliban militants. At the top of the hour, I saw a man in a dark suit mouthing absurdities. I glimpsed the Kabul skyline hovering over the blood-red chyron: *CNN Reporter Dead in Afghanistan.*

That night, I sat outside in my puffer coat and watched the meteor shower. Or maybe something else dazzled my eyes.

December 31: I arrive too early at my therapist's office. I can't be anywhere else.

Sylvia-at-the-front-desk ignores my wild eyes, says, "Take a seat, Paula."

I pick up the top magazine—*Science* or *Nature* or some other single-named periodical I always feel I *should* read but usually don't. I find myself failing to absorb an article entitled: *Double Trouble?*

It's not about meteors.

The little I understand indicates there are any number of binary star systems sprinkled across the galaxy. Sometimes one throws off too much heat and light, causing the other to overbalance and explode into nothingness. The first star, shocked out of its orbit, flies away on the ensuing shockwave. A runaway star, hurtling toward nothing.

Yo soy el Fénix

Sergio A. Ortiz

my multi colored feathers
shine. Your jailers
are no obstacle, it's my
nature to rise.
El tiempo me dice,
A jugado tanto con el amor
que ya no sabe amar. *
Camina, corre, cabalga.

Now what, where will you
go from here?
¿A que nueva cárcel
me desterrara?
¿A qué otro silencio? *

It pains me to know
that tomorrow's daylight
might bring you tears.

Niños del color
de mis tristezas jugando
frente al mar
en casa de cartón. *
Your choice, not mine.

Make sure you don't hurt
yourself while trying
to save me.

**He's played so much with love, he cannot love*
**What new prison will you exile me to? To what other silence Am I being banished?*
**Children the color of my sadness playing in a cardboard house in front of the sea.*

Disagreeing with Gandhi

Jessica Barksdale

Humanity is a dirty ocean
bobbing with bits
of plastic, fuel, and waste.
The whole world is an ocean,
says the cynic in her office
after a long pandemic
and a bad president.

Worse, she had a biopsy
yesterday in a spot
that makes sitting difficult,
and she is sitting,
writing to you now
from a place of irritation
and pain.

She is part of the world.
And she is dirty,
like her mother
is dirty. Her mother
is demented, too, living
in a comfort
she hates, and hating
her daughter, the one
who had the biopsy.

The world is on fire,
or soon will be, again,
summer forests containing
no moisture.
People have given
up on the pandemic,
forgetting death is on
the sidewalk waiting,
tapping his foot and checking
his watch.

Let us all go to the ocean,
let us walk into the surf.
Hear the gulls caw
their hunger. Step over
bits of plastic, twists
of dried kelp.
The ocean is dirty.
We are all part of the ocean.

Maelstrom

Adwoa Armah-Tetteh

Sanwaa remembered the first time she made the grass dance.

Heavy clouds hung in the sky, shielding the usually unmerciful sun. *Maa* had left her on the banks of the river to play with the other children as she carried water to their home. The other children ignored her, not caring much for Sanwaa who had only known one *harmattan*. Unperturbed, she crawled across the ground, incoherent sounds babbling from her tiny lips. A butterfly hovered into her line of sight, absorbing her attention. Pushing her hips back, her napkin-clad bottom met the ground as she reached for the butterfly. The butterfly was a frenzy of colours as compared to Sanwaa's dark complexion; the thought had saddened her but only for a brief second.

It was almost as if the creature was toying with her, whizzing out of reach each time her fingers caressed its wings. So they went—her chubby fingers grasping at air as the butterfly evaded capture. Unbeknownst to her, the other children had stopped playing and the women had stopped fetching water, calabashes slack in their grip. They watched wide-eyed as the grass surrounding Sanwaa rose and fell, bending and rising, as though bowing beneath the weight of the air.

Maa snapped out of it first, her clay pot falling to the ground and shattering into numerous pieces—they had to borrow Aunty Akua's own for a week; it had a hole at the bottom. She rushed towards Sanwaa, sweeping her into her arms. Sanwaa giggled, clapping wildly as the butterfly danced around her head. *Maa* turned to the other women, trying to come up with an explanation as to why her white-haired daughter seemed to control the winds. But it was too late, the women had already began whispering amongst themselves, one word constant—*beye*. Witchcraft.

Sanwaa remembered the first time she made the water move.

Daa had taken her fishing. It was against his will, his lips perpetually turned down in a frown—*Maa* had gone to visit her mother in the neighbouring village and everyone seemed to be busy that day. He didn't hold her hand like the other fathers did. But, Sanwaa didn't mind. She liked walking behind him and watching the sun bounce off his bald head which shone like a mud-coloured *asanka*.

Against the wishes of the other men, he had placed her onto the canoe. It had been a slow day for them. They cast their nets to either side of the canoe and yet caught no fish. Perspiration and anger lined their features. Sanwaa stood at the other end of the canoe, mindlessly humming under her breath, blissfully unaware of glances stolen in her direction and the complaints that stirred from deep within, slowly boiling over like *Maa's abenkwan*.

Daa, however, noticed—the curse of adulthood. With a resigned sigh, he gave the signal and they changed course, heading back to the shore. Sanwaa leaned over the edge, her fingers grazing the surface of the water. Something slid across her fingertips, glinting in the sunlight. Gasping, she jumped backwards. Curiosity edged her forwards, dipping her hands in the waters once more. She curled her fingers and the water followed, coating her hand like a second skin.

A dazzling grin broke out across her face. She opened her mouth to shout for her father when something glinted at the edge of her vision. Leaning closer, her eyes widened as she realised what it was. She whipped around, smile still intact. "*Daa, nam.*" Fish.

Eyes narrowed and lips drawn into a thin line, he shot her a look—the same one he gave her each time she stepped out of the house or they received a guest. Sanwaa of seven *harmattans* didn't know what it meant, but *Maa* always looked sad when she saw it. She called him over once more, pointing over the edge of the canoe.

The other fishermen ventured forward, gathering around the young girl. Her father pushed past them to where she stood, the remnants of his paternal instincts kicking in. Gripping the worn-out edge, he leaned closer to the water. When he saw no fish, he edged back slowly, head turning towards his daughter. "*Sanwaa.*"

There was no mistaken the undercurrents of anger, even Sanwaa knew that.

She groaned. *Daa's* sight had been failing him of late. She yearned for the waters to part so he could see the fish swimming about. Sanwaa reached into the water, hands moving as though trying to part it.

Shouts rose in the air and Sanwaa turned around, beaming with pride. *They had seen the fish*. However, *Daa* did not look as pleased as she had expected. His face was ashen, jaw slack. Sanwaa glanced back at the sea. The waters surrounding the boat had parted and the fish flopped on their bellies, bouncing off the dry ground. Sanwaa drew back as the shouts around her grew louder, one word echoing in her mind—*beyefuor*. Witch.

Sanwaa could not remember why she was awake so early.

Perhaps, she didn't know why. It was still dark, dawn more than a whisper away. Pale moonlight washed over *Daa's* face as he stood hunched over her, urging her to awaken. With a sigh, Sanwaa turned over to wake up her little brother—*Maa* did not like it when Sanwaa called him her brother; *Maa* had stopped liking a lot of things since *Maa* Efua moved in. But, *Daa* caught her hand, shaking his head. Then, as though her skin burnt him, he dropped it, recoiling backwards.

Rising from beside her mat, he gestured towards the cloth that served as a door, walking out of the room. Sanwaa followed suit, slipping her feet into her *chalewotte*, the heels of her feet touching the dusty concrete floor. The room had been swept the day before. It seemed as though her fourteenth *harmattan* was the harshest.

Daa led her outside. Two men stood there, arms crossed against their bare chests, strips of cloth tied around their waists to cover their modesty. Sanwaa suddenly felt conscious, standing there with a flimsy cloth wrapped around her. The men exchanged a few words with her father, stealing glances at her in between.

Sanwaa had never seen those men. Perhaps they were from the neighbouring village, seeking her hand in marriage. But, she had yet to do her *bragoro. Daa* had kept her entry into womanhood a secret, forbidding her from leaving the hut each time she bled. *Maa* had been very upset about his decision but there was nothing she could do—once *Daa* said something, it became law.

Their conversation came to an end, handshakes and nods going round. *Daa* stepped back and the two men walked towards Sanwaa, each one grabbing one of her arms and hoisting her upwards. Her head whipped from side to side, her terrified gaze falling on her father. "*Daa*?"

With each step that they took, her cries became more frantic, hands reaching out for her father. But he remained where he stood, unflinchingly watching as they carried his first child away, eyes narrowed and lips drawn in a thin line. Fourteen *harmattans* Sanwaa was more discerning and as the distance between her and her home increased, she realised her father would not be coming to her aid.

Twisting in the men's hold, she cried out for her mother, her throat going raw. One of the men dropped her arm, reaching into the side of his cloth. She yanked her other arm free and took flight, her cries growing louder with each passing second. People stepped out of their huts, eyes still bleary with sleep but minds sharp enough to understand something was wrong. They remained in their doorways.

Sanwaa's freedom was short lived. One of the men tackled her, like the way Uncle Kwesi tackled a runaway pig, slamming them both to the ground. Dust flew upwards, choking Sanwaa with each desperate breath she took. The man pulled her head backwards, shoving a handful of blue powder into her mouth. Through bleary eyes, she watched her father walk into their hut. The world went dark.

When she came too, an *abriwa* was hovering above her. Sanwaa scrambled backwards, her back hitting a wall with a resounding thump. The *abriwa* simply huffed, the wrinkled corners of her lips turned downwards. Leaning her stout frame against a thick cane, she peered closer at Sanwaa. She stood straighter, poking the young girl with her stick.

With a dismissive huff, she headed toward the door, cane dragging against the cement floor. Sanwaa sagged against the wall, reaching a hand to her aching head. Her throat was parched, dryness clinging to the inside of her mouth. Pulling her legs inward, she lifted her gaze to the cloth-covered hole at the pinnacle of the thatched roof, the only source of light.

Dragging herself to her feet, she rushed to the door, ignoring the increasing throb in her temples. She pushed the door, throwing herself at it, but it wouldn't budge. Body aching, Sanwaa slid to the ground, tears welling up in her eyes. And, she wept—wept for her mother, for her brother and for the knowledge that no one would be coming for her.

Sanwaa could not remember what it felt like to have the sun caress her skin.

She was kept locked up in the hut as days and nights bled into a continuous loop, one she could not follow. But the routine was the same. They would leave her alone for long hours on end, with nothing to keep her company but her deteriorating thoughts. Then, food would arrive, meagre scraps that would have been fed to the chickens back in her village. The food never tasted like food—at times it would smell repugnant, traces of unknown leaves hidden within. She could barely keep any of it down. Once she was fed, they would drag her out the hut and down to the lake and toss her in the deep of it. And while she flailed and cried out for help, the *abriwa* would watch from afar, chin propped on her hands which sat atop her cane.

And then, *it* would happen. The water would swirl around her, lift her and guide her to dry ground. The winds would whip through the trees, branches swinging, leaves rising and whirling in the air as Sanwaa gasped for breath. The *abriwa* would shake her head and the men would grab Sanwaa and throw her back in the hut. Each time she was tossed in, the time it took for her to return to the bank reduced and the frown on the *abriwa's* face would deepen.

Sanwaa lifted her head as a young girl entered the room, a single calabash in hand. A few feet away from Sanwaa, she dropped the calabash to the ground, kicking it the remaining distance. Sanwaa picked it up, frowning as a putrid smell rose from the food—a handful of rice covered in a green paste which was most certainly not *kontomire*. The urge to throw the food grew but Sanwaa squashed it, knowing nothing good would result. The men would force feed her whatever they could salvage from the ground.

Pinching her nose, Sanwaa tilted her head, downing the food in one go. Bile rose in her throat, but she swallowed, lips pressed tight against each other. The girl left the room, the guards swiftly taking her place, hauling Sanwaa off the ground and out to the lake. Momentarily weightless, she braced herself for impact, arms stretched, palms facing upwards. However, the water never came, the feeling of hopelessness did not follow.

Sanwaa hovered mere inches above the lake, air flowing around her like currents. A blissful smile crossed her lips. She urged herself towards the bank, letting out a laugh as the winds obeyed. The *abriwa* hobbled towards Sanwaa as the young girl settled on the ground, her expression grim. She gestured to the men to take her back to the room.

They had deposited Sanwaa in the room when the *abriwa* entered. Sanwaa frowned—that was not a part of their routine. In her hand, the *abriwa* cradled a familiar smelling concoction, the red liquid spilling over the sides with each unsteady step she took. She nodded to the men and they restrained Sanwaa. The young girl's heart began to race. The *abriwa* knelt before her, an almost morose expression on her face as she explained that since they could not *cure* her, they would have to ensure that she didn't pass the *beye* on.

It dawned on Sanwaa why the concoction smelt so familiar—it was the same one Aunty Yaa had taken when she and her husband had decided they didn't want any more children. She twisted in their hold, pleading with the *abriwa* and the men, to let her go, to stop the madness. After all, of what use was a woman who could bear no children?

The *abriwa* ignored her cries, kneeling down before the frightened girl, one hand squeezing her cheeks, forcing her mouth open. Rage, cold and unforgiving, washed over Sanwaa, evoking a sudden stillness. They had taken her from her family, starved her and abused her, but they were *not* going to take her unborn children from her.

Sanwaa's wrists rolled back, fingers flexing. She felt a tugging deep within her and leaned into it. The air seemed to buzz with energy as she drew her fingers closer, clenching them into a fist. The men's grip slackened, the *abriwa* reached for her throat, the calabash dropping to the ground. They all followed suit, eyes wide, hoarse rasps tumbling past their lips. Dark liquid tinged with red flowed from their mouths and eyes, darkening the spilled concoction.

Sanwaa would never forget the first time she drew blood.

Freckles

Shauna Clifton

A geometrical display of gold: bouquets of hay arranged
in the shape of a diamond. Everything shines, even the cows that face east;
a calf follows her mother; their coats glisten in the sun like water.
I am sorting cages for the queen bees, soothing myself in a rocking chair.
Yesterday, I pressure-washed the porch before placing potatoes in the oven.
Then, I planted blue plumbagos in the garden;
I needed oregano from the garden to go with the oil and butter,
but the porch was dense with water and leaves from another rain-storm.
I slipped and busted my knees; I noticed the porch's paint chipping away—
a dull red exposed like a blooming cut or puckered lips.
Lying on my side, I picked up an orange leaf to twist
its little disguise; its cuticle had been tampered with.
I realized that the faint dark spots weren't those of a leaf
but rather the freckles of a butterfly's wing.

Moon Maintenance

Arthur McMaster

Another thing you may as well know about the blues—they are not contained. Perhaps you would be surprised how far they travel. The Lady in the Moon must deal with them when they arrive, adding to her work: Bombs, blood, uncomely forms of sacrifice. And our constant wars down here cannot be said to be helping much: Rape, anthrax, landmines . . . The blind shards of artillery. She scrubs, she vacuums, she scours away, moving all the shit to where it cannot be seen—to the darker side—where not much shows. The old Man in the Moon cares not a fig for blues, nor scorched earth, nor any such bother.

Like most men, he looks after the larger affairs: Quietude. Normality. Prosperity. His white, round face beams benignly. And the tides roll in. And the tides roll out. Meanwhile, we, the more or less well-to-do, toss our year-end tell-tale woes into a churchly burning bowl. Smell the pretty pine. Feel the glow. Drink a toddy. Fondle something warm and supple. Where does all that refuse go? More work for the Lady. But, as we all know, it doesn't show. Carbon, radiation—like pesticides, they travel well. Three-Mile Island, Elk River, Prince William Sound, the Love Canal . . . The good Lady scrubs like hell, but there is so much to do. She moves all this too to the darker side. And the old Man yawns, scratches his balls. Chernobyl, Fukushima . . . And the tides roll in. Yes. And the tides roll out.

Dream Catcher

Elizabeth Christopher

There's a thud against the window, not as loud as a tennis ball's thwack, but still it startles me enough that I drop my pen and rise from my desk. I rush down the stairs as if toward a shrieking tea kettle.

A small bird's on our back deck. Black and white. This one must be a Chickadee.

I hurry back inside, grab one of Bill's shoeboxes from the mudroom, spill his new running shoes onto the floor, poke a hole in the cover with a kebab skewer.

I scoop up the bird. So light in my two hands it's alarming. It's all there: Feathers. Beak. Feet. How could something that weighs almost nothing make such a sound?

I sit down at the kitchen table with the box on my lap. It could be stunned, not dead. And if so, it needs a dark, quiet place to recover. I've read this before on the web. The first time a bird flew into our window was years ago, when the kids were small and they fluttered around these rooms. We lost a Blue Jay but saved a Sparrow. When the Sparrow came to, we went to the front porch and the kids set it free. I swear that bird cocked its head and winked at us, like something out of a Disney movie, before it flew away.

Last year Bill and I went on a killing spree. Snapped the necks of seven mice in traps we set under the kitchen counters. Bill set the traps, dabbed them with peanut butter, like we read on the web. I had gone along with it. More than that: I'm the one who discovered them. Found their feces in my muffin tins in the drawer under the oven, like some miniature game of Mancala. Also, they chewed through my bag of Raisin Bran. I emptied the bag into the trash and held it up to Bill. Said, *we have to get rid of them*. The hole they made was shaped like a sunburst. It was beautiful, in the way the artwork our children used to bring home from school was beautiful: surprising. Accidental. Like the tissue paper-stained glass and yarn-and-feather dream catcher I saved in the plastic tub in the attic. Whenever I lift the lid, the smell of crayon and watercolor rises from the box.

Our children live far away now. When they lived here, their presence felt heavy. They were always climbing into my lap, pulling at my arms. The air in these rooms was thick with their wanting. It was like gravity.

I write them letters at my desk in the room at the top of the house. The room is just for that, too small to be for anything else. Although I used to sleep there, back when Bill was having an affair. For months, I refused to sleep in our bed. That was a long time ago. The children were small, I was still young, and resentment came as easy as good muscle tone.

Now, something's living in the wall up in that room. Early morning, I can hear wings beating behind plaster and lath. It's likely a House Sparrow. How it had the strength to peck through soffit or fascia I can't imagine. What would I see if I took an ax to that wall? Small downy bodies huddled in a thatch of leaves and insulation? Acorn shards and dried out droppings? I won't spill the beans this time. I'll keep their fluttering to myself.

Our children's lives are full of other people now, of bosses, wives and mistresses, husbands and second husbands. Where my daughter lives, everything is bright and sharp. Palm trees. Prickly grass. Stucco walls. Spiked-back lizards. Her lawn is kept green by sprinkler systems and men who jump from truck beds once a week with their headphones and mowers. Without them, everything would dry out, turn back to desert. Why she wants to live in a place that's not meant to last, I'll never know.

Our children fly to places even farther away than they are now. Just last week our son sent us a postcard of turquoise waters and palm trees. I handed it to Bill who was icing his knees on the back porch. *Hawaii?* He asked, pinching it with his thumb and index finger. *Jakarta,* I said. He's a man now, our son, in finance. He was on a business trip. Received some kind of company award.

Bill took up running after the affair. Funny, I know. You'd think he would have gotten in shape *for her,* not after. He runs 30 miles a week, even now with arthritis in his knees. He could have run halfway around the world by now if he'd wanted to. Before Bill took to running, back when he was still having the affair, my son would climb the stairs to the attic at bedtime looking for the usual things from me: a story, a kiss goodnight. Such small demands; why did they feel so heavy?

One time, when I heard his socked feet on the stairs, I pretended to be asleep. I closed my eyes and lay still. His milky breath hit my ear. The chubby palms of his hands dawdled against my back. Only when he'd gone, did I turn and peek. There was his dream catcher next to my pillow along with a note in six-year-old crayon scrawl: *For good dreams momma.*

I open the shoebox and run my finger along the curve of the bird's back. I'm careful not to crush it; although, I know it's silly to worry about that. This one's not coming back.

Bill handed back the post card. *Indonesia,* he said, impressed. The card was as light as nothing, but still I had to place my hand on Bill's arm to steady myself.

1953 Miniature Train Driver

Amanda Trout

I set antique metal stool at the base of the conductor's car; I step and vault feet to driver's seat, pull button-lever and race the trees that always win this changeless track, and when the cars stop I vault back to standing speech, open gate, wave in patrons, lock gate, present smile that screams *I'm not afraid* loud enough to obscure vocal tremors, practice instruction, the art of welcome, of keeping hands and feet inside the cars, of all-aboard on three, of countdown, key-turn, of nervous impact speeding the heart, of one ear always open; I imagine clang of detached drive-shaft *press-button emergency stop breath steady*; I imagine child fallen on track *horn bellow bellow bellow* imagine emergency break too slow *bellow bellow*; I imagine dive from driver to savior, save the one and hope young adult bodies brake mini-trains quicker than dusty brake lines or sometimes I just sit in headlight horror and brace myself for impact.

Bringing Home the Bacon

Alice Lowe

1) Half a clove of garlic is never enough

A hundred miles apart, we alternated weekends between Redlands and San Diego, his place and mine. His cooking adequate but limited, I gave him *The New Pasta Cookbook,* inscribed it "A clove of garlic, a splash of olive oil, a sprig of basil . . . and thou," added a note: Spaghetti alla Puttanesca, page 48. If you make only one thing from this book, I said, let this be it.

> *Heat a generous glug of olive oil, add some crushed garlic, and sizzle slightly. "Some" and "glug" are arbitrary terms, as are smidgen and splash, dollop and dash. Recipes are guides—training wheels for novices—not laws to curb ingenuity.*

A friend brought me a purple t-shirt from the Gilroy Garlic Festival that read: *Half a clove of garlic is never enough.*

> *Add anchovies. Recipes say two, four, eight fillets—I don't count. Some say drain and rinse, soak them in milk to reduce the salt; I take them, salty and slippery, straight from the jar.*

You either love them or hate them—neutrality is impossible, compromise futile. He shared my fishy fetish and my garlic gluttony, promising signs for our future.

> *Stir in oregano and red pepper flakes until the aroma makes you swoon, a splash of red wine, a handful of Kalamata olives, a cluster of capers in their tangy/tart brine.*

Pour a glass of that red—I like Sangiovese—to sip while you cook. Absorb the ambience: the mellow wine, your warm and fragrant kitchen, an Italian tenor singing Puccini arias in the background.

Add a can of tomatoes (chopped or crushed); simmer and stir while the pasta cooks.

Add, subtract, or substitute whatever you fancy: onion, mushrooms, artichoke hearts, more seasonings. A white version uses tuna in place of tomatoes, white wine instead of red. Pasta puttanesca is said to have been created by prostitutes in Naples during World War Two, a quick dish using ingredients on hand, even in a brothel. Or a California bachelor's kitchen.

Now the finishing touches—a spoonful of pesto or tomato paste, a squeeze of lemon, chopped chives or parsley. Ladle over al dente pasta, top with grated Parmesan. Serve with salad, garlic bread, and more wine.

We merged and married after a four-year commuter courtship. Pasta puttanesca is a mainstay of our dining repertoire. I won't say food incompatibility would have been a deal breaker; I won't say it wouldn't.

2) Tortillas with butter

I took my daughter to the museums in Balboa Park to acquaint her with the abundant array of art, science, and history. She always begged, "Can we go see the tortilla lady?" In the lobby of the Museum of Man,[1] a woman in traditional Mexican attire patted balls of masa back and forth, flattening them between her hands. She browned them on a cast-iron griddle, buttered and wrapped them in paper napkins to hand to visitors. My daughter claimed more interest in this museum's exhibits—human skulls, headgear, and handcrafts—than the art museum's paintings or natural history's flora and fauna. I knew it was the tortilla lady.

[1] I later joined a boycott of the museum to protest its sexist name. It took forty years and a pandemic-induced budgetary crisis; now it's the Museum of Us.

My favorite Mexican restaurants are those that make tortillas in-house. Like El Indio, a San Diego institution since 1940, and Old Town Mexican Café, renowned for its carnitas. A friend gave me a tortilla press, and I learned to make my own.[2] Place a mound of masa on the metal plate, push the handle down to flatten it, cook thirty seconds on each side. I made tacos, tostadas, and enchiladas, but the tortillas were best straight from the pan, dripping with butter.

> [2] The novelty gone, the tortilla press abandoned,
> I buy tortillas at El Indio.

Living six months in a small English village, my partner and I drove to nearby Exeter for Indian and Italian dinners, to country pubs for English curries on cold winter afternoons or ploughman's lunches after vigorous hikes on the moor. The only thing we missed was Mexican food, scarce in thirty-years-ago rural England, where tortillas were sold in cans if at all.[3] Halfway through our stay a friend visited, bearing heaven cradled in a foam carrier—tortillas made just hours before she left San Diego. Heated and buttered, they tasted like home.

> [3] Mexican food is widespread in England now. It may not
> compare to what we enjoy here, next to the Mexican
> border, but a mediocre taco is better than no taco.

3) Bringing home the bacon

I don't eat meat, except for occasional bites of bacon filched from my husband's plate when we have breakfast out. During the Covid-19 quarantine, we bought a waffle iron to duplicate the waffles at Perry's, and my husband made challah French toast that rivaled The Mission's. But something was missing besides the restaurant ambience. It was with a furtive thrill that I slipped the first package of Trader Joe's Uncured Dry Rubbed Bacon into my cart. Now I buy a package every couple of months, rationing its fifteen slices over several weeks into:

1) Sunday breakfast with waffles, French toast, or pop-the-cardboard-can cinnamon rolls.

2) The classic BLT. Just B, L, and T on toast with mayo, a dash of Tabasco. Restaurants fancy it up with avocado and/or cheese, masking the pure bacon-ness of the smoky strips, the crisp freshness of tomato and lettuce, the creamy richness of the mayo.

3) Incomparable pasta carbonara: linguine tossed with beaten egg and Pecorino Romano, bacon bits fried to chewy/crisp perfection.

We're starting to eat out again. Now an occasional patio lunch, eventually we'll resume Sunday mornings at Perry's and The Mission. But there's no turning back—I'll continue to bring home the bacon.

Soaring

Michael O'Connell

The children launched themselves from the bus and formed their own galaxies on the playground, just as neutrons, electrons, and protons exploded outward after the birth of the universe. Most of the kids ran directly to the red and blue rocket ship slide, leaving swirling nebulae in their wake. The rocket towered over everything else in the yard and had all the best things to explore. It had multiple chutes—good to use as escape hatches if you needed to make a quick exit, monkey bars, and a swinging bridge. Usually, Terrie and Kevin would have been the first of the intrepid explorers up the ladder. They were smaller than the other kids, but they were also much faster. Today, however, Terrie, ever the one for exploring strange, new worlds, had an idea about how she might pull off just such a trip.

Kevin was sulking. "The swings are for the wimps and little kids, T. If you don't want to climb on the rocket, why don't we hunt for lizards or something? We might even get lucky and find a snake."

"Maybe next time," she said with urgency. Terrie had become obsessed with astronomy after her father went missing—after Don had begun to hang around her mother. It was one of the few things she could still remember about Daddy. She had tried to share her theory with Kevin that the pulsar she had recently spotted on her grandfather's old Celestron C10 telescope was actually her father. She had picked up some odd sounds, beyond the static, on Kev's CB radio, but he had scoffed. She remained determined. She had tried to adjust Kevin's Attitude Control System, but his ability to process such things was sorely lacking.

Terrie had gained the swing set. The structure was taller than most of its kind. And except for the vulcanized canvas seats, it was all metal. The chains were smooth, almost black down by the sling seat, as if charred from re-entry. Closer to the crossbar above, the galvanized chains had begun to rust. The swing set towered over the east end of the playground, and if it weren't for that fourth leg, it would have made the aliens of H.G. Wells envious. Terrie placed her hands on the chains, adjusted the seat, backed up, and then, just before she lost contact with the ground, launched herself—feeling the pull of Earth's gravity.

"Earth to Kev. If I'm gonna make this trip, you have to get over here and push."

Kevin lazily made his way toward Terrie. He looked past his friend on the swing and gazed at the starflowers where the tree frogs lived. They were just beyond the swing set, yet too distant. He could see himself tossing a few into Margaret Mary Dunn's hair—the wild, orange cluster orbiting her head. One day, he'd get around to it, and she'd learn not to be such a busybody. He could make out her wheezing laughter coming from the rocket. She was always louder than the other kids. He knew she'd be there telling them all to *Slow down* and *Wait your turn.*

"Kevin Ignatius Kelly. Anytime would be nice," Terrie said as she swung past again. The chains groaned like a Lovecraftian behemoth.

"Alright. Alright," Kevin said, as the swing set had begun making a low, rhythmic creak—the chains straining as the girl went higher.

Kevin lined himself up and waited for Terrie's descent back toward Earth. Then, timing the arc just right, he caught her by the seat and ran with her as fast as he could. Kev pushed with as much force as he could muster. The next time, he'd be able to duck under after he let go.

Terrie laughed. "That's it—just a few more times. I think I can feel . . . something . . ." As she made her transverse ascent, she saw the wood chips that were supposed to cushion your landing if you fell. She struggled to keep from dragging her feet through them as she passed. As she reached the end of the arc, she looked back toward Earth. Kevin looked so small. There was a faint shimmer to everything she saw, and, yes, she did feel something. The hairs on her arm were standing up.

"Just a little higher, and I'll make it. I'm almost there. I got my feet through for a second. It's so cold."

"Don't be a spaz, T." It was an active sun. Intensely bright. Kevin struggled to see her through the glare. He could almost hear his mother. Or was that Margaret Mary telling him not to stare into the sun, or he'd go blind?

Back down. Back up. Terrie continued on her pendulous, fractured orbit. Kevin grabbed his friend and ran hard one last time.

"Put some muscle in it. Push! Push! Push! I'm gonna touch the sky!"

Kevin launched her with as much force as he could muster, then ducked under and turned. He tried to look up through the sun's blinding rays in defiance of both his mother and Margaret Mary—right at Terrie and the sun.

"You're not Daddy . . ." he thought he heard his friend say. She sounded distant. Hollow and surprised. The sun seared Kevin's vision. He had to look away.

When the boy opened his eyes, he only saw a pulsing black hole where his friend had been. He heard the chains dance as he struggled to see. Slowly, his vision returned. And when it did, Terrie was gone.

Our Twilight

Jeanne Julian

Stepping outside, we watch
Jupiter chasing Saturn from east
to west across an indigo sky.

We find comfort in their choreography,
their set course eternal as the pursuit
Keats pondered on a fadeless Grecian urn.

Behind the planets, the vast marvel
of the Milky Way hangs invisible, glitter
vanquished by the city's conspirators of luster.

Pollution is christened like evil fairies:
Glare, Skyglow, Light Trespass, and Clutter—
counterforces recruited by a civilization

determined to dispel all darkness,
steal the night, make it our bauble.
Such vanity. Our human world

seems destined for a showdown
with fire, ice, and flood, leaving that urn,
"foster-child of silence," shattered or sunk.

Maybe then, stars will re-emerge, reflect in the widened surface
of deeper seas, unnamed but shining as if they could be admired.

Hero's Eyes

William Nuessle

Jessie tipped her gauntleted hand carefully so the peregrine falcon would step off onto the fence post and grip the wood with all eight razor-sharp talons. Heronimus settled on her perch, scissoring her blue-gray wings behind her back, studying her master with eyes of yellow-rimmed obsidian.

"We can do this," the falconer-in-training whispered to both of them.

She stepped away from the patient animal, drawing out fifteen feet of white, kite-string-like creance tied to the jesses attached to Hero's left leg.

"You tied her off with falconer's knots, I hope?"

Jessie forced a deep breath as she stepped back ten feet, keeping her eyes locked on the fence post. On her friend.

"You're going from that far? The first time?"

Another deep breath, eyes still locked. Hero was watching everything she did. This moment was critical. For balance. For trust. "This is not our agreement, Mother." With effort Jessie managed a low, even tone.

Movement in her peripheral vision as her mother stepped into closer Observation range, staying one step outside Interference. "Our agreement is that you're on your own, sink or swim; I never said I wouldn't monitor your progress."

Sink or swim, Jessie thought, reaching into a vinyl-lined pocket of her hawking vest. *Drown or fly, more like.*

If she succeeded, she would be a falconer, trusted completely with the life and care of the magnificent, medieval predator.

If she failed, she would be thrown to the U.S. Fish and Wildlife wolves as an untrained, unlicensed teenager harboring an endangered animal.

And said animal would likely be . . .

Jessie chopped this thought off at the roots. They weren't going to fail.

This was one of the moments on which everything hinged. No more thought. Action.

Pulling a gobbet of raw meat out of the pocket, she placed it in her gloved fingers where Hero could see and whistled *down-up-down* like they'd practiced over and over.

Without hesitation Hero leaned off the post, her talons scratching the wood. A rapid *whumpwhumpwhump* of powerful wings, a lifting of taloned feet later and Hero was feeding, the comforting two pounds returned to Jessie's wrist.

"Well done, my love," she whispered, elated. Rapid response was key. Either the falcon came or it didn't. The last thing Jessie needed was to screw up under the gimlet eye of Gloria Munoz, Owner and Director of Tacoma Bird Rescue.

One successful flight was acceptable. Even her mother would not, probably, fault her for calling it a day.

Jessie walked back to the fence post and tipped the falcon back onto it. "Go again?" she asked softly. Taking Hero's *pre-reet* as affirmation, she paced out twenty feet, the creance trailing through her fingers.

It was only as she turned, ready to whistle, that her mother spoke. "Your *quinceañera* next week."

Knowing the timing was yet another test, Jessie whistled *down-up-down*, her heart leaping once again as Hero flew toward her without hesitation. After the soft *thump* onto the gauntlet she gave the gorgeous creature her reward, only then looking at her mother. "What about it? Am I free not to come, somehow?"

While her mother chuckled at this, Jessie decided a third flight would be perfect. She walked back to the fencepost, running the possible matronly responses through her mind.

"You won't want the animal around so many people." Of course bringing Hero to a party wouldn't be a good idea. Didn't mean her mother wouldn't say it.

"Your father and I will be civil to one another on your special day." Likely.

"I'm so impressed by your progress with Heronimus I'll sponsor your falconer's license." Not likely.

Mother still hadn't made her declaration when Jessie turned back to her love from a full fifty feet away. It was a dangerous distance, falconer to falcon, pushing the envelope of her skills and their relationship. Hero shifted on the post. *You can do this, my love.*

Jessie drew breath to whistle as her mother spoke. "I've invited Irving."

Somehow she pushed *down-up-down* out through the immediate rage. She knew her mother had timed the statement to the millisecond, and that she had roughly two seconds to get herself under control.

Because, for the third time, Hero was winging her way eagerly. And the animal responded to her emotions. Should she find her accustomed perch shaking with anger the falcon might herself become angry, or frightened.

Frightened birds flew away. Jessie might be able to grab the long creance, or she might not. The fifty feet might get tangled in a tree, or it might not.

Months of effort would be wasted in any case.

So Jessie pushed it away, clamping down on the rage and the pain and the hatred. When Hero raised her talons and spread her wings, her accustomed perch was steady. Jessie released her breath with just a trace of shudder. "*Maravilloso, mi amor.*"

She looked in her mother's direction, not trusting herself to eye contact. *Satisfied?*

"You're doing very well, Jessica."

"I'm proud of you." She didn't say it. She never said it.

As her mother turned to leave the clearing, Jessie looked away, watching her peregrine feed, allowing herself to exult in the triumphant flights. Only one angry tear fell to betray her.

You came when I called. Nothing else mattered.

Nothing else mattered.

In the Last Year of Our Marriage

Jill Michelle

when the rains ceased
El Niño over
the cypress dome
on the farthest acre
of our homestead—
flooded under feet of water
for as long as we'd owned it—
held only puddles.
We walked the siphoned ground
astonished.
Where had it all gone?
Arriving at the lowest spot
we saw in a murky oval
no longer than a yardstick
and barely an inch deep
a pair of mudfish
miraculously alive
half out-of-water
thrashing
from side to side
holding on
to a world
already lost.

Creative Nonfiction First Prize

And The Road Goes On Forever: A Life On Two Wheels

Gerald O. Ryan

Glance past handlebar hands that grasp the long faint shadow cast in front of your bicycle in the early morning sunlight. See that gray silhouette transform from the gaunt Giacometti form on two wheels to a squatter combination of spinning circles and frame triangles as the sun rises higher in the sky. The shadow condenses, disappears as the sun reaches its zenith, now follows behind like a faithful dog for the rest of the day.

Look down and watch fading asphalt flow under rolling wheels. See knees and top tube and handlebar and arms joined in curious stasis and continuous revolution. The arms belong to the rider who belongs to the road that never ends. They've changed from smooth strong forearms to tauter drawn limbs, from the smooth skin of youth to the complex alligator map of wrinkles that so absorbed a young boy as he studied his father's arms as a child. See the knees now scarred from surgeon's knives, protesting as the road continues, but still faithful to the rider who knows them well.

Look up and see parallel lines ever retreating toward the teasing horizon or the next hill, down tree-lined paths and corn-filled country roads, always approaching the next town or rest stop, always receding into thin memories as you rejoin the road.

Roll past far-spaced farms, neat boxes of white houses and rickety red barns. See newborn kids and calves. Smell hogs and fertilizer. Hear the sounds of tractors turning the soil for the fresh planting of crops, the sound of harvesters at season's end as that bounty is reaped. Wave and be waved at by the solitary occupants of huge farm combines as they rumble down that same shared road.

Pedal down stretches of towering green pines that coolly exude rich resin aromas. Coast and hear the tick of the freewheel in the oddly quiet calm and stately forest silence. Hear the tap of woodpecker and watch the sudden flit of the cardinal. See the squirrel as it darts from tree to tree in never-ending, nut-carrying mission.

Ride by the river and peer through early morning mists and rough stalked reeds to see fish jump and fowl preen. Smell the curious, rich odor of decay where water meets bank in marshy confluence. Inadvertent inhale and swallow swarms of bugs that dance at the river's edge.

Careen down city streets, ever alert, always surprised at the car-bus-truck that leaps in front of you with no warning. Immerse yourself in traffic sounds and diesel smells, in potholes and pedestrians, in stop lights and swung-open car doors. Hear the constant honk and roar. Feel your hands grip the brake levers in sudden stop.

Places may change, but the road goes on forever.

Feel the seasons roll by, the never-ending wheel of spring, summer, autumn, winter, the forever cycle of years that will continue long after bicycle wheels cease their spin.

Pedal through new buds and the creeping green seen only from the corner of the eye until spring bursts forth in sudden surprise all around you. Creatures court and birds build nests among blossoms and slowly warming air that caresses and calls you back to the road after a long lonely winter.

Immerse yourself in endless wheat which waves in summer winds. Watch black asphalt shimmer and dance in distant mirage. Feel the sweat drop from forehead to top tube as you cycle, heat making skin glisten, sun's rays darkening arms and legs in that curious cyclist's tan. Taste the lukewarm water as it wets dry lips and somehow satisfies parched mouth. Sway in the saddle with Tiger Lilies and Queen Anne's Lace that roadside bow in constant courtesy. Hear the whirr of locust chorus that sing their familiar song, rising and falling in Doppler mystery as you pedal past.

Tilt your head at the hint of the first dropped leaf and be amazed at the abrupt autumn riot of orange, red, yellow, and brown. Arms and hands hide under jackets and gloves as you pedal through dimly lit mornings and frosty air. Watch your breath condense in moisture-filled exhalation. Hear ducks and geese honk over your shoulder as they make their way south.

Worship at the window while winter snows blow and hide the road as it disappears outside in swirling fury, leaving you with only well-worn maps and fading photographs of remembered rides. Sleeping legs will phantom pedal, twitching curiously like a dog's in rabbit-chasing dreams.

The seasons change but the road goes on forever.

The road is a constant that's ever different but always the same, somehow new and somehow not. It's a way through life with limbs moving in continuous revolution, endlessly approaching but never arriving. Because whenever you look up from handlebar hands and spinning legs, from burning muscles and labored breath, from sudden thought or bittersweet memory, you always see the road that goes on forever.

Prose Poetry First Prize

car wash orgasmic whirl

Nicole Farmer

For only five dollars fed to the off-road robot, wheels lock into the wet shimmering drag system, neutral gears sucked into the bubbling bliss, leaving the world behind as me and my vehicle are mechanically pulled into a cave of cleansers and cacophony of motion. Seat tilted back to the maximum spaceman oblivion, radio rocks John Lee Hooker into my pelvis. Deep exhale as the water and light skate across my windshield dancing over my half-closed eyes; jaw-jiggling jelly roll for me and my old jalopy. Purple popping bubbles turn caterpillar green psychedelic liquid lava luminescence as giant rag eggbeaters pound the sides of my old gypsy wheels, shimmy shake me to shambles, expel us new and dripping, birthed into blinding brightness. Machine and mistress emerge cucumber clean, optimism in every turn. I call that a middle of the week miracle.

The Healing Wave

David Partington

Despite having just returned from three months at a wellness retreat in Florida, Elliot Hope needed a good, stiff drink. Unfortunately, there was no alcohol in the house, and no cigarettes either, those habits having been left behind, along with the hustle and bustle of the 1990s, when he went to the retreat. Therapists there had recommended physical exercise for stress, so he grabbed an old jacket from the hall closet and headed out for a walk.

Upon reaching the sidewalk, he took some deep breaths, reminding himself not to 'catastrophize,' then turned to face the cause of his distress: in the middle of his front lawn, a large, lovingly-planted flowerbed, which on this spring day should have been resplendent with crocuses and bluebells, had been trampled. From this vantage point he noticed for the first time that the footprints were quite small, like those of a child, and that the trampling hadn't been random, rather it spelled something: "T-Y-L-E-R."

With his blood pressure rising, he began marching down the sidewalk. It was one of those sunny days in March when the thawing earth releases the unmistakable smells of spring, and the tall trees lining the street, most still without leaves, rise to meet a clear blue sky. But it wasn't any of this that suddenly made Elliot smile; rather he was 'raising his vibration' by looking on the positive side of things, just as his life coaches had told him to. Lacking the self-confidence to question life coaches—or anyone else—he thus rejoiced that he didn't know young Tyler because if he did, he would undoubtedly wring his scrawny neck and be jailed for homicide, or at the very least land the urchin in the hospital and then go on trial for attempted manslaughter. On the other hand, if he stayed calm, he might be able to sue the boy's parents for damage to his property or compensation for mental suffering. The thought of the child and his parents in a courtroom begging for mercy was strangely soothing.

Elliot's first job was clearly to locate this Tyler person. He had always avoided his neighbours, fearing they might judge him, but now he needed to talk to someone. Near the end of the street he came upon a red-haired girl, probably about fifteen, mowing the lawn in front of a yellow-brick bungalow.

With his right hand in his jacket pocket, he felt a loose cigarette from his former smoking days, but he resisted the urge to pull out and smoke, his social anxiety having, for the moment, been supplanted by indignation.

A divorced, middle-aged insurance executive, Elliot knew nothing about young people beyond what he'd read about them in the *Saturday Evening Post*, yet with his temporary boost in self-confidence, he was able to go up to the girl and speak.

The willowy teen held up a finger, mouthing the words "Just a sec!" then finished mowing the last strip along the boulevard.

"Mowing the lawn?" asked Elliot.

"No—doing the Macarena," she replied.

Brushing aside her sarcasm, he introduced himself as "Mr. Hope from down the street." The girl said that she was Lara.

Wasting no time in small talk, Elliot asked her directly if she was aware of any small children in the area.

"Just my little brother Tyler," she said.

"Ah! That's the one!"

Lara turned and faced Elliot directly. "Look, whatever you think he did, he didn't do it."

"No? What makes you so sure?"

"Well, what do you *think?*" she said, placing her hands on her hips. "Unless you've been living under a rock, you can probably guess."

Though taken aback by the girl's impertinent manner, he patiently explained that he had indeed been away for several months, and though not actually under a rock, he was little out of touch. "You can't imagine how I've suffered!"

"Whoa! Are you *serious*?" She lowered her sunglasses and looked at him with apparent compassion.

"Yes, *quite* serious!" Before revealing Tyler's atrocity, he endeavored to lay out his struggles with stress and blood pressure, and his recent stay at a retreat, intending to lay the legal groundwork for his case of property damage and mental anguish.

"Okay, but here's the thing," Lara interjected. "Tyler can't have done anything because of his medical condition."

"Medical condition?!" said Elliot, feeling as if a rug had been pulled out from under him. "Oh, I'm so sorry! Is he confined to bed now?" Flustered by his miscalculation, Elliot reflexively pulled out his one cigarette and put it in his mouth.

"No, he's not here. They had to treat him for Schwartz-Ostein Syndrome."

"Oh—the poor child! I feel terrible now!" With trembling hands, he started fumbling through his pockets hoping to find a lighter. "Which hospital is he in?"

"Actually, he didn't go to the hospital. Quite the opposite."

"The opposite of a hospital?"

"Yeah—the Rock and Roll Hall of Fame."

"I don't understand. Surely that's no place for a sick child."

"I'll tell you all about it," Lara said, pulling a lighter from the pocket of her pink track pants and handing it to Elliot. Ordinarily, he would have wondered why someone so young was carrying a lighter, but at that moment he was simply grateful. "Just let me unplug this thing." She went off to unplug the lawnmower, leaving Elliot to focus on his cigarette as he tried to regain his composure.

"So you're sure you haven't heard any news in three months? Nothing at all?" Lara asked as Elliot handed back the lighter.

After he assured her that he knew nothing and didn't even own a computer, much less Windows 98, Lara explained that her brother been critically ill—"It was touch-and-go at one point"—and that he'd gone to the Rock and Roll Hall of Fame thanks to the Make-a-Wish Foundation. "He got to see one of Phil Collins' drumsticks and a dead Tamagotchi that had belonged to Hootie!"

"Hootie?"

"From Hootie and the Blowfish."

"Ah."

"Anyway, the highlight came at the end of the day when the rest of the public was gone and Tyler was taken to see a pair of sequined pants worn by Britney Spears in one of her videos," she said, now pulling the cord across the lawn and winding it into loops. "The guards who stood by the glass showcase put away their guns and opened up the front so Tyler could touch one of the hems. It was just for a few seconds, and just his thumb and first two fingers, but they were the actual pants!"

"The *actual pants*," repeated Elliot in wonderment. "I guess that was quite a privilege."

"A *privilege?* Are you kidding?! It was life-changing! Tyler was cured!"

"What?! How can that be?"

"It was a miracle. Somehow the spirit of Britney entered Tyler through the pants and drove out his medical issues. That's what experts are saying."

"Holy smoke!"

"And the rest is history!" said Lara.

Flicking an ash, Elliot reminded her again that he'd been cut off from news sources. "So what happened next?" he asked, leaning back against a lamp post.

"Well, obviously he became famous after that. At first, it was just a few print interviews, but after he brought someone's cat back to life, everyone started freaking out, and it turned into this whole big *thing*. Now everyone wants him for his healing powers."

"So you're saying he can now heal others?!"

"Well, Tyler's too modest to take credit for any miracles; he says he's just become a channel for Britney's pants."

"And he actually brought a cat back to life?"

"That's what they say. The only other explanation is that the family found another black cat very similar to the one that had died a few years ago. Anyway, the cat showed up the day after Tyler had ridden his bike past their house, so that tells you everything. And get this: some English guy presented a paper on the subject to The Royal Society, and now he's going to be knighted or something. Crazy, huh?"

Elliot exhaled a long slow stream of smoke, then shook his head in wonderment. "No kidding." Engrossed in the story, he was now breathing slower. "So where is Tyler now? Is he at home?"

Lara suddenly looked him over with suspicion. "Hey, are you a reporter or something?"

"Of course not."

"Because you ask a lot of questions!"

"I'm just curious!"

Lara made a little sneer then continued, explaining that Tyler had been moved to an undisclosed location for security reasons. "But all that was like two months ago. Ever since the business with the cat, there have been all these other miracles and healings—one thing after another. Needless to say, Tyler had to stop dealing with fans directly—so no more photo opportunities. We don't want a bunch of geeks staking out the house hoping to catch a glimpse—and we *certainly* don't need more paparazzi! You see that Girl Scout over there?" she said, looking over Elliot's shoulder. "Never mind—she just ducked down behind the hedge. She's probably from *The National Enquirer*."

"Not a real Girl Scout?"

"No. Too big. Plus, she looked like a dude. And remember, for every 'Girl Scout' you see, there are probably seven or eight more hiding in the bushes."

"Isn't there some way of deterring them?"

"Well, no one's allowed to report on him directly because of National Security or something, so all the Tyler news is between the lines. Plus, there's a sniper on the roof over there. Officially there isn't, but I'm pretty sure there is." Elliot began turning around. "No—don't look!! Geez! Do you want to get us *killed?!!*"

"Sorry."

"Of course, Tyler doesn't believe in merchandising, so you won't see Tyler lunchboxes or anything like that. I've seen people wearing the letter 't' on a chain around their necks, but those were never authorized. What can you do, right?"

Elliot nodded sagely. "I guess when something good happens, there'll always be people trying to make a buck."

"You got that right! If people want a bit of Tyler in their life, their best bet is to buy a 'Sheet of Paper That Has Been in The Same Room As Tyler,' though those are getting hard to find."

As she spoke, Elliot's eyes widened; he raised his arm wordlessly and pointed at a black cat crossing the sidewalk.

"Yup—that's the one!" said Lara. "Looks pretty alive to me. You couldn't ask for more proof than that!" She had finished winding up the cord in big loops and now slipped it over the handle of the lawnmower.

"So what about you and your parents; do you still see Tyler?"

"Not really. It sucks, but his life has become too big for ordinary folks like us. Though three weeks ago his motorcade passed in front of the house."

"His motorcade?"

"Yeah. We couldn't see his face, but as his car went by one of the tinted windows rolled down far enough so that he could stick out his hand. He has this trademark gesture where he holds up his thumb and first two fingers—the ones that had touched the pants," she said, making the gesture with her raised right hand. "It's too bad, but I have to remind myself that he's not just my brother, he's *everyone's* brother. He's no longer a particle in space, he's more like a wave—a healing wave. That's what what's-his-name, that science guy in the wheelchair said. I'm not trying to make it sound spooky, but now he moves on such a lofty plane—it's like he has this omniscient spirit."

"So does he at least communicate with your family?"

"Oh, no," said Lara, now wheeling the lawnmower back to the garage as Elliot walked alongside. "Well, actually yes. It's kind of freaky; he gives us signals sometimes. If you ever notice a jet flying overhead at night with a flashing light, that's a message from Tyler saying all is well. And sometimes when Dan Rather ends the news, he'll hold up his thumb and first two fingers, Tyler-style. That means Tyler says 'hi.'"

"That's strange," said Elliot, tossing his cigarette butt over the neighbor's fence.

"Well, you know Dan Rather . . ."

"No, I don't."

"Exactly."

They had now reached the open garage, where her mother's car was absent but which was filled with crowded shelves that smelled of motor oil and fertilizer. "Of course," Lara continued, "there are always *sightings* of Tyler, but those are just what they call *apparitions*. You know, people think they see him playing in a ditch or knocking over a mailbox—stuff like that. They say it always foreshadows some sort of good fortune."

"Oh!" said Elliot. "You'll never guess what I saw today!" He told her about Tyler's name appearing in his flowerbed.

"No way! Now *that* is something!" Her expression turned serious and thoughtful. "I mean, it doesn't surprise me that he would bless your house like that; he must have sensed you were, like, stressed or whatever, so he sent you his benediction." She gazed at Elliot almost reverently, then turned her eyes toward the sky. "May his spirit never cease working its wonders."

Choked with emotion, Elliot thanked Lara profusely, assuring her once again that he wasn't with a news organization and that he would be discreet and not do any interviews. As he turned to leave, Lara called him back to the garage, where she held a piece of blank paper.

"Here," she said. "You can keep this." She placed the paper in his hands. "Tyler would want you to have it."

Elliot understood the significance of the gift and thanked Lara again before heading back down the driveway. "Mr. Hope," Lara called after him. She was holding up her thumb and first two fingers. Beaming from ear to ear, he returned the gesture, then went on his way. He didn't need a cigarette, and would doubtless never need one again. Clutching the paper to his chest, he inhaled the uplifting smell of newly mowed grass.

Lara's mother brought Tyler home from soccer practice at the usual time that Saturday afternoon. Tyler was annoyed when Lara made him promise to stay out of other people's flowerbeds but soon got over it. In the years that followed, there would be many more occasions when he would be grateful for his older sister's imagination.

Father's Day

Jean Harper

The last time I see my father it's in memory
care. He's finishing lunch, alone at his table,
a napkin protecting his wrinkled shirt, the gray
plate before him scattered with flakes of salmon.

He's anchored into his wheelchair, leaning over his food,
his fingers tools he can't remember how to work.
Hi Dad, I say, and he raises his head and stares at me,
and I know he knows he doesn't know who I am.

The napkin over his shirt is gray like the plate
before him and the last of the pink irretrievable fish.
Now, a merciful girl turns my father's chair around—
Activity hour, someone reading trivia questions, A to Z.

My father raises his head, stares at this alien person.
I know he doesn't know if this is a game or something else.
What one of these every day keeps the doctor away?
What has nine innings? Who says meow?

That girl is mercy itself, patient beside my father's chair
and me through the full alphabet of trifles and questions.
Only one tiny man is really playing, shouting answers as fast as
he can before they disappear: *Baseball! Oranges! Daughters!*

What is the opposite of less? What time do you eat lunch?
What will make you weep when you cut it open?
Now my father is sleeping, oblivious to everything—to the game
at last closing in on X and Y and Z, to me beside him, to time itself.

The tiny man stands up, calling answers so they won't disappear
Red Sox games! When it's orange! My daughters!
This is the last day I remember seeing my father and he is finished
with lunch, and breakfast, and everything else. We are all alone.

Now my father sleeps, oblivious to everything—
games and questions, language and daughters, time itself.
Now, my father has put out to sea, tilting toward the horizon,
his hands working the memory of fathomable tools.

Tea Leaves and Muddled Midnight Messages

I dwell in possibility ~ Emily Dickinson

Jennifer Grant

Dear Emily:

Tonight, my beloved coerced me to binge watch a television show depicting you as a rebel scribbler with 21st century sensibilities. I prefer period pieces infused with more than shards of truth. But I'm clutching my chipped cup of Womankind Tea brewed with cranberry, rose, and vanilla, witnessing your desire for unfettered femininity to birth velvet petal words that bloom with your mood.

Did you know your name translates to *striving* or *eager*? Mine loosely transmutes to *fair one*. Whether it refers to my freckled skin's fragility or post-menopausal mind, I do not know. I'll sift through the tea leaves of similarities between us and convert them to slant rhyme come sun-up.

Living in pandemic isolation, my lyric seams unraveled, unlike your stitched-tight verse. You published 10 poems during your lifetime. My first collection printed when I turned 50. Now as I inch toward your death age, I too consider answering the door to delivery drivers while wearing a white dressing gown.

I was born 73 miles from your Amherst home. Does that make us kin? My current panhandle drawl would not fit with refined New England literary salons. I have a sister Suzie, once my most trusted confidante. Your Sue swapped you for your brother. My Suzie replaced me with one daughter who shares your first name and another she christened with your saintly middle. Maybe if I rename my heart Emily and strive for sanity, I will be saturated in poetic ingenuity rather than lukewarm tea.

Cyclist

Anne Whitehouse

On my bike, I am leaving the park, down shuttered side streets, across the avenues' uneven intersections. I listen to the bump and whir of my wheels against the asphalt. I pass blunt-topped towers between shafts of darkness.

My shirt flares behind me, and I am straddling the narrow seat, pedaling fast as the street inclines gently down. The buildings grow smaller, older; fire escapes criss-cross their faces. Figures blur past me as if in a dream: a man on a grey concrete stoop drinks from a flask, a woman leans from a window, two boys jump towards an orange ball poised in a ring. Their shouts meet me like a hot wind, and I travel through them.

Past patterns of scaling walls, doorways that open to darkness, I lean, and the bike turns; the street reflects fish-eyed in a pool at the base of an opened hydrant. A cloud shifts in that black liquid. Behind me, the sun is lowering; its warm streaks caress my back. Again the street has changed; its surface is a smooth black glass, obsidian. I see that I am approaching the shores of a river of sorrow. Every morning the sun flees from it. Down there a man plays an accordion; a dancing monkey is waving his cup. Rats sleep in the splintering wharves; the benches are bolted into place.

But all moves away from me, all disappears in the bicycle's receding wake. I turn away from the shadowy river. An elderly man points his cane at my spokes. "So the silver spiral unwinds," he says, "into its valley at last." And the street opens.

A street of single houses from a century ago: brown sea stone cut in blocks, black gates of wrought iron, and window boxes where the velvet petals of geraniums bloom in utter stillness. The hooks of questions prick me: I am slowed; I stop and walk the bicycle, a finger laid across the handlebars. At first it seems the only living thing on the block is the light that slides across the windows. It catches each afire, burns, and leaves a crystal. Depths open in the glass. I am looking into a room: a study, a library. Ever so slowly, I slide past in the windows, while the light from across the sky turns the brown stones pink. The heart of a rose smokes in them, a stain of ash on the sidewalk. The spokes of my wheels are dulled to the lustre of old pewter.

Here I am unknown; no one misses me in the glistening windows. A breath of mist on a table: wiped away, does the street exist? I have stopped; I am sitting on a step, drinking water from a plastic bottle. My bicycle leans on an iron gate. Even when I close my eyes, I cannot hear the breeze lifting the hair from my neck. And when I open them, the light is deeper and the shadows of clipped hedges wave across the stones. In the room above me, a pen scrapes over paper and someone hums a lullaby from long ago.

And yet the song is not from the room after all. A little girl is singing it, and she is coming down the street towards me, balancing a large metal hoop with a stick. She beats it lightly to her rhythm—tap, tap, tap. Then gravity accelerates it, and she hurries, it slants an oval down the street; her thin legs make shadows like the bicycle's spokes. Her hair is dark silk, waving like a fringe, hiding her face, as she looks only at her hoop. In the world only her hoop exists, and the song she is humming. It passes me in snatches like thoughts said aloud. In spite of her running, she is a long time coming to me: her feet clatter on the walk like rain on the roof of a country house; her hoop is a swish of wind.

And when she reaches me, she looks up and her eyes meet mine. Blue-grey, immeasurable distance. I gaze steadily back, not blinking. I am rooted to the stoop like the geranium to its box. She is so close to me that her features dissolve, and only her eyes, a child's clear eyes, fill my vision. Neither of us speaks. I feel the air touching my eyes, I feel naked. I know without looking that the hoop is perfectly poised; with only the top of her stick touching it, it balances on an infinitesimal point like a world stilled.

Her eye is like a pearl washed by changing light yet itself changeless. It is then, when I am almost lost in her look, that she speaks. Her voice catches as it surfaces; it is as ragged as the grass trampled in the park, as the torn streets I have travelled. "Do you know me?" she says, and waits, and her mouth crumples. I am afraid she will cry.

"No," I say, "I have never seen you," but she has not lingered: mirrored in the windows of silent pink-brown houses, she runs with the whirling hoop down to the end of the street, towards the river, where it is already dark.

Contemplation

Barbara Dobrocki

we step on the sunlit meadow
arena of woods' sizzzzz hum
cicadas' rapid buckle and unbuckle of drumlike tymbalas

trees cast deep shadow coolness
their squirrel-tails waving over the tall grasses swaying
sizzzzz males' love songs

strewn aromatic pine needles mounds
with varied weather-worn wood markers
sizzzzz Elysian Fields?

each site peeks a brass spike from its center
with a circular top engraved name date of birth death
sizzzzz frenzy Aristotelian and Iroquois delicacy

bio-degradable benches
wood bird houses scattered
female cicadas die after laying hundreds of eggs

I tell my husband when it is my time
wrap my body in organic cotton cloth
sizzzzz fast heart beats of loved people left behind

bury me here by the southern pine
near lush flora of blazing star tickseed milkweed
peace of wild things

an adjacent field teems with feeding
dragonflies swirling in a placid blue sky
some Chinese eat cicadas symbolic of rebirth and immortality

rest a large piece of nature's sculpted wood
at the head of my gravesite
sizzzzz hum fades at dusk

Fiction First Prize

Huitzilin

Tomas Baiza

Sunlight pools, trickles, and then begins to spill over the edge of the mesa. No sooner am I reborn than I am drawn to it, as I am drawn to the flowers that grow in my father's yard. Sun and nectar, *Tonatiuh* and *xochinecutli*, both of them fuel for the returned warriors, we who have been summoned to face our shames before being called to fight.

In the kitchen window, my reflection, an orange spark and wings that slash like the flint knives of our ancestors, the obsidian blades that opened veins of eternal life onto the tongue of the Sun Stone.

Tonatiuh

For all of his lovable bullshit, Papi was right about You.

He pushes himself off of the mesa and takes flight, His golden river now a roaring whirlpool of fire. The universe bends under His weight, falls upward. I feel His pull.

no, por favor, todavía no

Not yet.

Beneath me, my father's prized red valerian, the only thing that would grow in the sour soil beneath the kitchen window. I dip to drink, its delicate blossoms the shade of my mother's too-bright lipstick that she would wear even when gardening. Twist, bend, attack, retreat—every flower an invitation to violence or love, my blurred wings fed by their essence.

Tonatiuh kisses my black beak. My eyes flutter with His call.

Not yet. Please.

I am distracted by a flash. A rival. Another warrior called back. We spin and joust. Our kissing shrieks bounce off the kitchen window. I sense that she, my adversary, has already served her purpose, made her peace.

But I have not yet made things right.

She retreats to a high branch of the massive honey locust that my father would call *ese pinche arbol de mierda*—that piece-of-shit tree—for all the leaves it would drop, impossible to clean, our rakes useless in the high-desert autumn. But now it is full and green, a perfect redoubt for my rival.

Through the window, I can see clearly into our kitchen. A large jar of *agua de jamaica* is cooling on the table.

Papi makes *jamaica* for Mom every Saturday.

I spin to glare at my rival. *¡I am home!* I shout.

¡No time! she chirps from her branch. *¡He is rising!*

no, todavía no

Next to the wall phone is the calendar that the *panadería* gives its most loyal customers every January.

"Papi," I asked him once, "how come the calendar shows the *dieciséis de septiembre* but not the Fourth of July?"

My father looked up as he stirred my mother's *agua de jamaica*, a wry smile twisting his brown face. "Porque a los mejicanos de México no les importa ni papa la independencia de gringolandia." *Because the Mexicans of Mexico don't give a crap about* gringolandia's *independence.*

"Well, *I* don't give two shits about all the Saints Days," I shot back. "You can tell the Mexican-Mexicans that for me."

My Papi's shoulders shook in silent laughter as he stirred the deep red tea. "Jíjole, m'ija," he said, "eres una furiosa."

And, if the unfamiliar holidays and religious holidays weren't enough, the calendar would feature monthly depictions of *nuestros antepasados*, our ancestors. Aztec stuff, like the scenes on all the lowriders that bounce past at every Cinco de Mayo Parade. Chesty goddesses swooning in the arms of feathered warriors carrying them up the steps of a pyramid, saving them from the jaws of flying serpents, wresting them from the grasping hands of Spanish Conquistadors. A dozen Salma Hayeks prostrating themselves to a dozen Benjamin Bratts.

"Do you *really* think that's what our ancestors looked like, Papi?" I asked once. "Don't you think any of us were fat or ugly or dorky? I mean, didn't any of them have big foreheads or underbites or hammer toes?"

Papi took a sip of tea from the spoon and nodded. "A lo mejor." *Maybe.* "But some myths are worth believing in, *m'ija*."

Every thought of Papi threatens to send me plummeting to the ground from shame. Only *Tonatiuh* lifts me and drives me to my last task before I go to fight forever.

The calendar says July. A square in the middle of the month is circled in red pen. I press as close to the window as I dare, my wingtips brushing the glass.

July 16. The year . . .

My wings falter, even the towering Sun can no longer hold me up. I plunge into the red valerian, cradled in its velvety leaves. My rival chirps in alarm.

Four years since the accident. Of course.

My father's stick-thin arm shook as he braced himself against the kitchen counter. "M'ija," he said, "have I ever told you about Huitzilopochtli?" Since the chemo, his eyes had become sunken and yellow, like old lemon rinds poking out of the dirt.

"No, Papi. You never mentioned *Wee-tsee-lo-whoever*," I said. Can you go to hell for an eye roll?

"Pues, mira," he said, his voice breathy from the strain. "He was the Lord Chuparrosa, the Hummingbird of the South. Tonatiuh himself."

"¿A mi qué, Papi?" I said. *What's it to me?* I couldn't look at him. Those sunken cheeks and sagging eyes. I couldn't decide which frightened me more: the radiated husk of his face, or the defiant grins on the days he felt the worst.

"It's just . . . I'm trying to teach you," he said. "When we leave this world, He waits. He is patient. Your abuelita taught me that He lets us rest for exactly four years to the day and then brings us back to help Him. Since the beginning, *m'ija*, He honors us as *huitzilin*, as hummingbirds, His most honest and loyal warriors."

"Why are you saying these things?"

Papi pushed himself along the counter toward me. He took my face between his shriveled palms. "Because I want you to know that I'll be back, for a little bit, after I'm gone. Your abuelita always said that He gives us one chance to say goodbye before we go to war, the real war, the one He fights every night to be able to return to us in the morning. He only chooses the strongest." Papi smiled at me, the pride bringing a temporary flicker to his hollow eyes. "Only His chosen ones are allowed to make things right one last time before they serve Him."

"God, Papi!" I yelled. "You can't seriously believe that superstitious shit!" I hated him—for being sick, for making me miss him before he was gone, for trying so hard. And now for going crazy. Wasn't dying enough? Did he have to do it insane, too?

I ran from the kitchen to the garage and slammed the car door before he could catch me, frail from the radiation. He pulled on the door handle and tripped alongside the car as I pulled into the street. I watched him shrink in the rearview and gasped through the tears when he fell, sprawling on the pavement.

How could I have done this, leaving him face-down on the street, weak and alone? I raged at my cruelty and cowardice.

Blind to the curve in the road, I screamed as the car broke through the guardrail and tumbled into the canyon.

A whirring nearby, past the blossoms. *He calls. ¡Get up!* My rival's wings stir the leaves above me.

I rise. The Sun bounces from my feathers, blood-orange jewels dazzle in the kitchen window's reflection.

She retreats again to her branch. *¡Hurry!* she warns.

I know she is right. With every minute, the roar of *Tonatiuh's* fire grows louder, more irresistible. Through the glass, I glimpse a shadow in the hallway, beyond the kitchen. I throw myself at the window.

My companion screams from her branch.

Again, I crash into the glass.

Tonatiuh-Huitzilopochtli's voice vibrates through the light. *You are of no use to me broken, little one*, He says.

I dash myself against the window a third time. Movement in the hallway now. Papi totters into the kitchen, that bemused look on his face that always made me giggle. He is bent, but his cheeks are full, his eyes open and alert.

Alive. My Papi is alive.

I turn to let the Sun dance off of my feathered armor. I lift my beak to the sky. My companion answers from her branch. A shared war cry.

Papi steps up to the table and places his hands on the large glass jar, testing the *agua de jamaica*.

I spin and whirl, throw my most furious poses, but he does not notice. My warrior blood froths at the snub. *¡I am home!* I shout. *¡I am here!*

Papi lifts the jar and begins to turn away.

I speed at the window, heedless of my tiny body or my companion or *Tonatiuh* or the coming battle. The glass cracks with the impact and I tumble, crashing through the branches of the red valerian until I fall through to the dirt below. From the honey locust, panicked chirps. Far above, *Tonatiuh-Huitzilopochtli* groans. My tiny leg hangs limp beneath me, but my wings are still sharp. They lift me again and the Sun's call is stronger than ever. My companion's shrieks are blood-thirsty and feral. She is close to giving in.

no, todavía no

Papi peers wide-eyed through the window, his face haloed by the spiderweb crack I have left in the glass.

I rise before him. My armor glows fierce in the light. Despite my broken leg, I bob, I weave, I thrust and parry for him. *¡See me!* I bellow. *¡I am strong!* I hover in the chill morning fire and then approach the window. My father and I stare into one another's eyes.

¡I am sorry!

Papi jerks back, trips against the table. The jar of *agua de jamaica* falls and shatters at his feet spraying steeped hibiscus across the floor. I am drawn to the crimson sweetness almost as strongly as I am to the Sun.

Slowly, my father turns to face the calendar. He extends a trembling hand to the middle of the month and rests his finger on the third Saturday of the month, circled in red marker. The day of the accident. Eyes sparkling, he stares back at me through the cracked window, proud tears lining his cheeks.

Behind me, my companion hovers, her beak glinting in the Sun. *It is time. We must go to Him.* She is right.

Tonatiuh-Huitzilopochli floods the yard with His light. *Come, Little Ones, my furious yaotiacahuan, my precious jade warriors. Take your place among us*, He sings.

I lower my beak and gently, carefully, press my orange head against the window. Papi lifts his palm to the glass. For a moment we are still, the only movement my blurring wings.

I love you, I chirp, and pull away.

If this was my penance, my duty, then the coming battle is my reward. As if shot from a bow, my companion arcs skyward, no longer able to resist His call. She becomes a tiny mote against *Tonatiuh-Huitzilopochli's* golden face.

I rise into the light and look down, one last time. Papi is standing on the back porch now, his robe flapping against his skinny legs in the dry morning breeze. Through his tears, he yells, fists raised in the air, his face radiating love. I toss my head back and let loose a cry that would make eagles cower—regret, anger, shame, but also pride, courage, redemption. I aim myself at the Sun. I race upward to the only war that was ever worth fighting.

Above the Sun's roar, Papi's last shout comes through. "¡Arriba, m'ija!"

And so, I become light.

After the Harvest

Scott Ragland

In New Delhi, beggars and bankers cough into masks and curse the smog mottling streetlights along Sansad Marg.

In Rania, Kuldeep and his daughter Baljit come in from the fields and sit playing chaupar at the kitchen table. Kuldeep wins the first game but not the next. He smiles.

"Your mother would be proud," he says.

He rolls up the board, careful not to fray the fabric.

Baljit watches him for a moment, then looks out the window. The rice stubble smolders now, smoke billowing skyward, scudding south on the wind. She blows, as if to hurry it on.

A young man from the government arrives, wearing a tie, clean-nailed, shirt sleeves rolled to the elbows. He hands Kuldeep a piece of paper picturing machinery. "A 'Happy Seeder,'" the young man says. "Pull it behind your tractor. It turns stubble into mulch as it furrows the fields, to enrich the soil as you plant your winter wheat. A better yield and more money for you. Cleaner air for everyone."

"Burning kills the rats," Kuldeep says. He looks at the pictures and calculates the cost of fuel to pull the metal's weight. "And I can't afford it."

"The government will help," the young man says.

Kuldeep gives Baljit the paper to take to the waste bin. "My father needed only me," he says.

After the harvest, Kuldeep would gather a pile of rice-shorn stalks. His father would give him a box of matches, and he would wait for a wane in the wind, then strike a match, touch it to the pile and rake the stalks into the fields. He would watch the flames spread like sinners loosed from the hells of Naraka, the distant rosewoods shimmering through the rising heat.

At dinner, his father would talk of the British Raj, of the Skull Famine centuries ago in Madras, the millions dead, the bodies piling too fast to burn or bury, the bones whitening roadsides and empty pastures.

"Never again," his father would say.

He would talk of the "Green Revolution," of rust-resistant wheat strains and tractor-plowed rice fields that spread to cover Haryana's plains like carpets in a prince's palace. He would talk of a nation feeding itself.

"We saved us all."

Kuldeep shows Baljit how to sauté onions in sunflower oil to mix with rice and cinnamon, like her mother had done. They eat and do the dishes, Kuldeep scrubbing clean, Baljit toweling dry, the air still flush with the meal's aroma.

They play chaupar. Then, before going to bed, Kuldeep watches Baljit play a computer game. A cartoon heroine scampers up scaffolds and leaps across flying islands, wields a flaming sword and scatters clouds of magic dust. Baljit asks her father if he'd like to join her.

"We could take turns," she says.

Kuldeep laughs, defers to getting older, the creep of years and time-dulled synapses, but still watches, cheering when another foe falls.

Kuldeep coughs in the night, waking Baljit in the next room.

"Are you OK father?" she asks, her voice reaching through the wall. "You sound like mother."

"I'm fine," Kuldeep says. "Go back to sleep."

He feels his wife's empty place beside him. He listens to his daughter's silence in the darkness, wondering how long it will last.

In the morning, smoke still obscures the sky, the smell like pus from a wound in the earth. Kuldeep pours wheat seed into his drill machine. He can see Baljit at the edge of the fields, digging through the ash with a plastic shovel. Kuldeep tells her to fetch the government paper from the waste bin.

"Put it with the chaupar board," he says, "to remind us to look at it together."

The day after her father's cremation, Baljit rises at dawn and takes the train east to Haridwar, where the Ganges tumbles from the Himalayan foothills. She scatters all but a handful of her father's ashes in the river's sacred water.

Returning home, the train stops to refuel at a cluster of mechanical trees on the city's outskirts, their leaves of plastic resin unfolded to catch the carbon on the wind, their steel converter tanks glinting beneath the high-noon sun. Baljit can see the attendant monitoring the pressure gauges and remembers the first time her father let her fill their tractor with diesel and start the engine on her own. She remembers her mother lifting her up to sit in his lap. She remembers turning the key and the rumbling rattle of pistons coming to life like a beast awakened. She remembers steering the tractor into the fields, her father's guiding hands covering hers on the wheel.

Baljit arrives home as dusk gathers, the sun sinking behind the rosewoods. She sits at the kitchen table, the chaupar board unfurled in her father's place, and watches a video on her computer about grid-free solar panels that absorb light at every latitude, about batteries that propel aircraft over oceans. "Not a dream for tomorrow, but a reality for today," the narrator says. "UN subsidies of up to 50 percent. Free delivery, installation and retrofits for your combustion engines. Join us in a Green Revolution for the 21st century."

Baljit places the order and goes to the fields. She holds her father's last ashes for a moment, then blows, letting the wind carry them away. She watches as they descend, whispers of gray vanishing amidst the wheat-seeded furrows. The rosewoods' shadows lengthen toward her. She waits for the first star to appear above.

Poetry Second Prize

Key Lime Pie

Shoshauna Shy

This surge of happiness with the orange poppies
blooming in my skirt, the glass beads in a shimmy
down my wrist, how my limbs feel supple and sturdy
after the hills I've bicycled for a week gives this day
a *Chelsea Morning* soundtrack because of the tabby

I spot prowling among the ferns with her symmetrical
ankle stripes; the blueberries that are my breakfast,
and because I just got word that the tedious series
of meetings with a neighborhood foe, concocted by
an alder candidate who lost, has finally concluded.

Lantana crawls through my garden with the intent
to decorate, and the kalanchoe with its triple bouffant looks
like it's celebrating the sky, and dear God, everybody
doubts you exist when another snubbed American male
sprays a school, a theatre, a hot yoga studio with bullets.

I prefer to think you are as devastated as I am; that when
Anne Frank's diary was yanked from her hands and pitched
against a wall as if into oblivion, you were the one to rescue it;
that you neither create nor condone evil, but like me wither
in sorrow at its strength. I like to believe you applaud when

we slice a piece of key lime pie in forgiveness, splash beauty
on canvas, reach out to someone in tears. Believe you are beside
me in my joy the way when last December, my dead father joined
me beside a Christmas tree, soft and soundless as the purest love
he hadn't shown in years, so here I am, strapping on sandals

to pedal yet another bicycle into yet another summer,
sunlight filtered onto my path, and all the maples laughing.

Bacopa Poets & Writers

2021

Ardsheer Ali is a marketing professional by day, lonely writer by night, whose work has been rejected by the *New York Times, Narrative Magazine*, etc., and who's written a full-length novel that is now lying in the slush piles of every major publisher.

Rebecca Anderson is a psychotherapist and fiction writer who is working on her MFA in creative writing at Mississippi University for Women. She lives on a small farm in central Maine.

Adwoa Armah-Tetteh, born and raised in Accra, Ghana, is an eighteen-year-old medical student. During her free time, she likes to get lost in her imagination, penning on paper the storylines running amok in her mind.

Tomas Baiza was born and raised in San José, California, and now lives in Boise, Idaho. He is a Pushcart-nominated author whose short fiction and poetry have appeared or are forthcoming in *Parhelion, Writers in The Attic, Obelus, In Parentheses, Meniscus, [PANK] Magazine, 101 Proof Horror, The Meadow, Peatsmoke, The Good Life Review, Kelp, Black Lawrence Press*, and elsewhere.

Jessica Barksdale's fifteenth novel, *The Play's the Thing*, and second poetry collection, *Grim Honey*, are both forthcoming in April 2021. Recently retired, she taught at Diablo Valley College in Pleasant Hill, California for thirty-two years and continues to teach novel writing online for UCLA Extension and in the online MFA program for Southern New Hampshire University. Born and raised in the San Francisco Bay Area, she now lives in the Pacific Northwest with her husband.

Claire Bateman is the author of eight poetry/prose poetry collections, with another, *Wonders of the Invisible World,* to be published in October (42 Miles Press). She is also a visual artist.

Steven Beauchamp is a retired English professor emeritus from Perimeter College at Georgia State University where, for some years, he edited poetry for the college's literary journal, *The Chattahoochee Review*. Over the years, he has had 100+ poems published in journals and reviews across the country. Currently he splits time between Atlanta and Port Charlotte.

Wendy BooydeGraaff's poems have been included in *Not Very Quiet, Local Honey|Midwest, South Broadway Ghost Society, Nymphs*, and her prose is forthcoming in *The Dribble Drabble Review* and *TERSE*. Her short fiction has been nominated for both the Pushcart Prize and the Best Small Fictions anthology.

Helen Bournas-Ney was born in Ikaria, Greece, and grew up in New York City. She received the Anaïs Nin Award for her work on Rimbaud and George Seferis. Most recently, her work has appeared in *Plume Online, The Ekphrastic Review, One Sentence Poems, Mom Egg Review – Mer Vox*, and the anthology *Plume Poetry 7*.

Shuly Xóchitl Cawood is an award-winning author. Her books include *A Small Thing to Want: Stories* (Press 53) and the memoir *The Going and Goodbye* (Platypus Press). She teaches memoir and personal essay workshops. Learn more at www.shulycawood.com.

M. Cynthia Cheung is an internist who trained at the University of California, Los Angeles, and currently practices hospital medicine in Texas. Her writing has appeared or is forthcoming in *Sugar House Review, Zócalo Public Square, The Journal of the American Medical Association, Modern Haiku*, and *Hawai'i Pacific Review*, among others.

Elizabeth Christopher writes and lives in the Greater Boston area. Her stories and essays have appeared in *The Writer, HuffPost, Obelus*, and elsewhere.

Shauna Clifton quotes Montaigne: "The continuous work of our life is to build death." Her voice derives from reading voices that have explored the many and ambiguous paradoxes of humankind, including the obsession to create. Her voice thus far describes her surrounding world and the sorrow that sometimes hides beneath what can be deemed beautiful.

Selena Cotte is a poet/writer/shapeshifter with work in/forthcoming from *Landfill, Tiny Molecules, Maudlin House, Hobart* & other journals. She grew up a few miles from Disney World.

E.H. Cowles, a retired social worker, lives and writes poetry in Gainesville, Florida. He enjoys performing his poems at open mic events hosted by local poetry groups, both past and present, including University of Florida Poets, Art Speaks, DopenMic, Mellow Soul, Artist Village, Melrose Community Poetry, and Civic Media Center.

Kym Cunningham, having earned her MFA from San Jose State University in 2016, is currently pursuing her PhD in English with an emphasis in Creative Writing at the University of Louisiana at Lafayette. Her current work examines the confluence between poetic spatialities and linguistic de/construction, being especially indebted to the labor of radical Black feminists. Her debut essay collection, *Difficulty Swallowing*, was published by Atmosphere Press in 2019.

Matthew Dettmer studied English Literature at Marquette University and then medicine at the Medical University of South Carolina. He is a writer, musician, and physician currently practicing in Cleveland, OH. His work has been published in *The Harpy Hybrid Review, Olney*, and *The Gravity of the Thing*.

Barbara Dobrocki is a visual artist, retired art instructor, fledgling poet, and a member of the Writers Alliance of Gainesville's poetry pod, Inkwights.

Les Epstein is a poet, playwright and educator whose work has appeared in *Clinch Mountain Review, Mojave River Review, Fourth & Sycamore*, *Jelly Bucket*, and is forthcoming in *Slant* and *The Bluestone Review*. Finishing Line Press will publish his chapbook *Kip Divided* later this year.

Nicole Farmer is a writer, teacher, and director living in Asheville, NC. Her poems have been published in *The Sheepshead Review, The Bangalore Review, The Roadrunner Review* and *The Great Smokies Review*, and her play 50 JOBS was produced in Los Angeles. As a child, she dreamed she was a superhero named Jaques who rescued damsels in distress with no cape, but with a fantastic mustache.

David Gambino is an MFA student at the University of Mississippi and an Air Force veteran. "Cold Eggs" is a work of fiction. Every sentence is true.

Jennifer Grant resides in Gainesville, FL. Her first collection of poetry, *Good Form*, was published by Negative Capability Press (2017) and a tiny chapbook, *Bronte Sisters and Beyond*, by Zoetic Press (2018). Her chapbook, *Year of*

Convergence, was published by Blue Lyra Press (2020). She was recently named winner of the 2021 Blue Light Book Award for her manuscript *Dangerous Women.* jenniferlynngrant.com

Atreyee Gupta explores the liminal spaces in which humans interact with society, geography, and identity. Atreyee is the creator of Bespoke Traveler, a digital alcove for curious travelers. Atreyee's work has been published by *Arc Poetry, Blue Cubicle Press, Rigorous, Jaggery Lit*, and *Shanghai Literary Review* among others.

Patrick Cabello Hansel is the author of the poetry collections *The Devouring Land* (Main Street Rag Publishing) and *Quitting Time* (Atmosphere Press). He has published poems and prose in more than 70 journals, including *Bacopa Literary Review*, and has received awards from the Loft Literary Center and MN State Art Board.

Jean Harper's writing has appeared in *The Florida Review, North American Review, Iowa Review*, and elsewhere. She has received fellowships from the National Endowment for the Arts and the Indiana Arts Commission, and has been in residence at Yaddo, MacDowell, and the Virginia Center for the Creative Arts.

Amie Heisserman is a Pacific Northwest writer with an MFA in Creative Writing from the Northwest Institute of Literary Arts. She has studied with Carolyne Wright, David Wagoner, and Ana Maria Spagna. Her work has previously appeared in *Bacopa Literary Review*. Learn more at amieheisserman.com

Holly M. Hofer has lived in north Florida most of her life and she's glad to call it home. She grew up in Gainesville, studied literature and programming in college, and currently works in the building controls and engineering field. She's been published in *Welter, The Avenue,* and *The Flagler College Review.*

Mirela Hristova is a multilingual literary translator and the owner/director at AMAT-AH Publishing, Sofia, a recipient of many literary awards, a Scottish Art Council Translation Fellow and Literature Ireland's Translator in Residence. Although many brilliant writers are read in Bulgarian in her translations (Terry Pratchett, Edna O'Brien, Maggie O'Farrell, to name but a few), this is the first time she has expressed herself as an author.

Máiréad Hurley moved from the UK to North Carolina a few years ago, where she works in data entry and attends Guilford Technical Community College.

Jeanne Julian of South Portland, Maine, is co-winner of Reed Magazine's Edwin Markham Prize (2019). Author of *Like the O in Hope* and two chapbooks, she has published poems in *Comstock Review, Kakalak, Poetry Quarterly, Naugatuck River Review*, and other journals. She reviews books for *The Main Street Rag*. www.jeannejulian.com

Alec Kissoondyal is a student at the University of Florida. He is currently pursuing a bachelor's degree in English. He is a writer for *Narrow Magazine* and an ambassador for the Florida Hemingway Society.

Sandra Kolankiewicz's poems have appeared widely, most recently in *One, Fortnightly Review, Otis Nebulae, Galway Review, Trampset, Concho River Review, London Magazine, New World Writing*, and *Appalachian Heritage.*

Adam Knight is a writer and teacher in northern New Jersey. His debut novel, *At the Trough*, was published in 2019 by NineStar Press and his fiction and essays have been published in a number of publications. His story "Hoping for Red" was published at *Escape Pod* in December 2018. He is currently revising a cosmic horror novel about the Titanic.

Jennifer Lang's essays have appeared in *Under the Sun, Ascent*, and forthcoming in *Consequence*, among others. A Pushcart Prize and Best American Essays nominee, she holds an MFA from Vermont College of Fine Arts and serves as Assistant Editor for *Brevity*. Born in the Bay Area, she lives in Tel Aviv, where she runs Israelwriterstudio.com.

Frederick Livingston plants seeds in the liminal space between food justice, ecology, and peace. His work has appeared in literary magazines, academic journals, public parks, and bathroom stalls. Compelled by the power of metaphor to shape our world, he hopes to share in telling new stories.

E. D. Lloyd-Kimbrel has been writing something of one sort or another since childhood. Over time, in-between employments, academic endeavors, and geographical locations, through cats, marriage, peonies, and early widowhood, she has published biographical, critical, personal, and scholarly articles and essays, and a scattering of poems in little literary journals.

Alice Lowe writes about life, literature, food and family in San Diego CA. Recent essays are published in *Burningword, ellipsis, Parhelion*, and *Epiphany*. She's been cited in Best American Essays and nominated for Best of the Net. Read her work at www.aliceloweblogs.wordpress.com.

Kurt Luchs (kurtluchs.com) has poems published or forthcoming in *Plume Poetry Journal, The Bitter Oleander*, and *London Grip*. He won the 2019 *Atlanta Review* International Poetry Contest, and has written humor for the New Yorker, the Onion and McSweeney's Internet Tendency. His books include a humor collection, *It's Funny Until Someone Loses an Eye (Then It's Really Funny)*, and a poetry chapbook, *One of These Things Is Not Like the Other*. His first full-length poetry collection, *Falling in the Direction of Up*, was recently issued by Sagging Meniscus Press. He lives in Portage, Michigan.

Carolyn Martin is a lover of gardening and snorkeling, feral cats and backyard birds, writing and photography. Her poems have appeared in more than 130 journals throughout North America, Australia, and the UK. She is the poetry editor of *Kosmos Quarterly*: journal for global transformation. Find out more at www.carolynmartinpoet.com.

Janet Marugg writes from Clarkston, Washington. She enjoys gardening, fishing, kayaking, reading and writing–all with her husband and dogs. She is an active member of the Idaho Writers League.

Sarah McCartt-Jackson is a Kentucky poet, folklorist, and educator. Her poetry books include *Stonelight, Calf Canyon, Vein of Stone*, and *Children Born on the Wrong Side of the River*. She has served as artist-in-residence for Great Smoky Mountains, Catoctin, Homestead, and Acadia National Parks.

Jonathan McLelland lives in Tuscaloosa with his wife and two sons.

Arthur McMaster's poems have appeared in *North American Review, The Worcester Review, Rhino, and Southwest Review*. His latest book of poems is *The Whole Picture Show* (Revival Press, 2021). He has one Pushcart Prize nomination and is now a retired English professor (Converse College)

Linda McMullen is a wife, mother, diplomat, and homesick Wisconsinite. Her short stories and the occasional poem have appeared in more than ninety literary magazines. She received Pushcart and Best of the Net nominations in 2020. She may be found on Twitter: @LindaCMcMullen.

Jill Michelle teaches at Valencia College in Orlando, Florida. Her poetry and creative nonfiction have appeared or are forthcoming in *The Cypress Dome, The Fox Hat Review, Wizards in Space, Please See Me, 86Logic, Sutterville Review, Paper Dragon, Halfway Down the Stairs, Prospectus,* and *Delmarva Review*, among others.

Fern F. Musselwhite is a lawyer and writer, raised in Massachusetts and settled in Florida. She published *Windblown*, her first novel, in 2019. Fern enjoys sports, travel, and running along shady trails deep into the forest.

William Nuessle holds a third-degree brown belt in ninjitsu, rides a Harley, primary caregives three small boys, and claims he can recite the alphabet backwards in less than ten seconds. He also writes occasionally.

Michael O'Connell, a retired creative director and illustrator, has danced about the publishing industry for decades. Currently, he enjoys writing and working hard at retiring. He lives in North Florida, is at work on his first novel and will finish soon, thanks to acquiring professional help.

Jeremiah O'Hagan lives and teaches in Washington state. His students are broken and beautiful, like we all are.

Somo Ihezue Onyedikachi is a writer living in Logos, Nigeria. He likes the smell of rain.

Sergio A. Ortiz, retired English literature professor, bilingual Queer Poet, founding editor of *Undertow Tanka Review*, Pushcart nominee, Best of the Web nominee, and 2016 Best of the Net nominee, won second place in the 2016 Ramón Ataz annual poetry competition. Recent credits include *Maleta Ilegal, Indolent Books, HIV HERE AND NOW*, *Communicators League*, *RatsAssReview, Spillwords, The Maynard* and other publications. His chapbook, *Welcome To My Archipelago*, will be published by Paragon Press.

David Partington is a newly retired zookeeper who has taken up short story writing as a pandemic pastime.

Mandira Pattnaik's work has appeared or is forthcoming in *Best Small Fictions 2021, Flash: International Short-Short Magazine, Atlas & Alice, Citron Review, Watershed Review, Passages North, Amsterdam Quarterly, Bangor Literary,* and *Timber Journal,* among other publications.

Scott Ragland has an MFA in Creative Writing (fiction) from UNC Greensboro. His flashes have appeared in or are forthcoming in *Ambit, The Common* (online), *Fiction International, the minnesota review*, and *Brilliant Flash Fiction*, among others. He lives in Carrboro, N.C., with his wife Ann and two dogs.

Shana Ross bought her first computer working the graveyard shift in a windchime factory, then spent a good while authoring a stable life before finally turning her attention to the page. Her work has appeared in *Chautauqua Journal, Ruminate, Bowery Gothic, Kissing Dynamite, SWWIM* and more. She is a past Parent-Writer Fellow at MVICW, and serves as an editor for *Luna Station Quarterly*. She rarely tweets @shanakatzross.

Rae Rozman is a poet and educator. Her poetry, which often explores themes of queer love (romantic and platonic), loss, and education, has been published in several literary magazines and anthologies. You can find her on Instagram @mistress_of_mnemosyne sharing poems, book reviews, and pictures of her rescue bunnies.

Gerald O. Ryan wrote columns for the Courier Sun, Windy City Sports, Chicago Amateur Athlete, and Liberty Suburban Chicago Newspapers. His poetry is published in *The Prairie Light Review* and he won the Mountainland Publishing Poetry Grand Prize and best U.S entry in the Fifth International Poetry Contest in *Firstwriter.com Magazine*.

Timi Sanni is a Nigerian writer who is fond of experimental writing, with works previously published in *Palette Poetry, The Temz Review, Lucent Dreaming, X-R-A-Y Literary* and elsewhere. Winner of the SprinNG Poetry Contest 2020 and the Fitrah Review Short Story Prize 2020, He is also a recipient of the NF2W Poetry and Fiction Scholarship.

Gianna Sannipoli's poetry has been published in *The Cardiff Review, London Grip, The Seattle Star, Mason Street, The Wild Word, Panoply, One Sentence Poems, Dodging The Rain, Red Coyote, Otis Nebula*, and Gnashing Teeth Publishing's anthology: *Love Notes You'll Never Read*. She is the Poetry Editor for *San Antonio Review*.

Claire Scott is an award-winning poet who has received multiple Pushcart Prize nominations. Her work has appeared in the *Atlanta Review, Bellevue Literary Review, New Ohio Review, Enizagam* and *Healing Muse,* among others. Claire is the author of *Waiting to be Called* and *Until I Couldn't.*

Shoshauna Shy's poems have been published widely, made into videos, displayed inside taxis, and plastered onto the hind quarters of city buses. Author of five collections of poetry, she is the founder of the Poetry Jumps Off the Shelf program, and the Woodrow Hall Top Shelf Awards.

Dutch Simmons established a creative writing program for his fellow inmates while incarcerated for a white-collar crime. Nominated for the PEN/R.J. Dau Short Story Award, Pushcart Prizes, and for the Texas Observer and Julia Peterkin Flash Fiction Prizes, he is a fantastic father, a former felon, and a Phoenix rising.

Travis Stephens is a tugboat captain who resides with his family in California. An alumnus of University of Wisconsin-Eau Claire, recent credits include: *2River, Sheila-Na-Gig, Hole in the Head Review, GRIFFEL*, and *The Dead Mule School of Southern Literature.* Visit him at: zolothstephenswrites.com.

Lora Straub (she/her/they/them) lives in Boston, MA. Her poetry prose chapbook, *Id Est,* was released in October 2017 by SpeCt! Books. Her work can be found in *Construction Mag, She Explores, The Fem, The Elephants,* and *Wave Composition*, among others. She is currently working on a memoir.

Amanda Trout is an undergraduate student at Pittsburg State University majoring in Creative Writing and Spanish. Her work has been printed in several publications, including *Cow Creek Review, The Lyric*, and *littledeathlit.* She was a poetry finalist for the 2021 Lex Allen Literary Festival and nominated for a 2021 Rhysling Award.

Anne Whitehouse is the author of seven poetry collections, most recently *Outside from the Inside* (Dos Madres Press, 2020), and a novel, *Fall Love.* Recent honors include 2018 Prize Americana for Prose, 2017 Adelaide Literary Award in Fiction, 2016 Songs of Eretz Poetry Prize, 2016 Common Good Books' Poems of Gratitude Contest, 2016 RhymeOn! Poetry Prize, 2016 F. Scott and Zelda Fitzgerald Museum Poetry Prize. She lives in New York City. www.annewhitehouse.com

Megan Wildhood is an erinaceous, neurodiverse lady writer in Seattle who helps her readers feel genuinely seen as they interact with her dispatches from the junction of extractive economics, mental and emotional distress, disability, and reparative justice. She hopes you will find yourself in her words as they appear in her poetry chapbook *Long Division* (Finishing Line Press, 2017) as well as *The Atlantic, Yes! Magazine, Mad in America, The Sun*, and elsewhere. You can learn more at meganwildhood.com.

Danae Younge is a rising sophomore at Occidental College whose work has appeared in more than 20 publications across the US, UK, Canada, Pakistan, and internationally, including *Salamander Magazine, The Curator*, and *Invisible City*. In high school she was selected as a 2020 national winner by The Live Poets Society of New Jersey.

Bacopa Editors

2021

Mary Bast's creative nonfiction, poetry, and flash memoir have appeared in a number of print and online journals, and she's author, co-author, or contributor to eight professional books from her career as a psychologist, leadership consultant, and Enneagram coach. Bast is also a visual artist.

J.N. Fishhawk is a poet and freelance writer. He is the author of two poetry chapbooks and *Postcards from the Darklands*, ekphrastic poems accompanying artwork by artist Jorge Ibanez. Fishhawk and illustrator Johnny Rocket Ibanez published their first-in-a-series children's book *Billy & Tugboat SallyForth* in 2020. Info at fishhawkandrocket.com.

Kaye Linden holds an MFA in creative writing. Her works include novels, short story collections, and manuals, including *35 Tips for Writing a Brilliant Flash Story* and *35 Tips for Writing Powerful Prose Poems.* She has just published her second novel, *The Beekeeper's Twin,* and is currently working on *35 Tips for Writing Memoir in Short Stories*. Visit Kaye at www.kayelinden.com.

J. Nishida holds a BA and MA in English, an EdS, and a TESOL graduate certificate. She has been, in her time, a library story lady, public school teacher, college writing instructor, ESOL teacher, editor, arts advocate, writer, and mom. She has spent a lifetime studying literature, poetry, mythology, folk tales, linguistics, languages, and translation.

Stephanie Seguin writes fiction and humor that have appeared in various journals and anthologies. Currently she is trying her best to write and exist while raising two small children in a pandemic. Some of her past work can be found at www.stephaniesays.net.

Made in the USA
Las Vegas, NV
14 October 2021

32374878R00111